The Way Out

The Way Out

Retracing America's Steps to Find Our Future

By

Bradford F. Whitman

The Way Out
Retracing America's Steps to Find Our Future

Published by: Bradford Whitman Books

For more information, please contact the author directly at:
bfwhitman2@gmail.com

ISBN: 978-0-9977087-0-7

Editorial services provided by:
Stephanie J. Beavers Communications

Cover design provided by:
Biddle Design

In memory of my late father-in-law, Nicholas Biddle Jr., who loved and honored the republic, in peace and in war, and inspired all of us.

Contents

Preface

A half dozen years ago I attended a ceremony to dedicate a moot, or simulated, courtroom at a public high school in Philadelphia, Constitution High. Constitution High is only a few blocks from Independence Hall, the birthplace of America, and the National Constitution Center. At the dedication former Supreme Court Justice Sandra Day O'Connor and Circuit Court of Appeals Judge Marjorie Rendell presided over a mock trial by the high school students. The level of energy and enthusiasm and the degree of preparation, sincerity, and respect exhibited by these young students was impressive—qualities that have long been on the wane among practicing lawyers and legislators, even judges.

Justice O'Connor touched briefly upon the meaning and importance of civics, the subject now taught at Constitution High. (Civics and civility have the same Latin root: citizen.) Civics and civility have disappeared from America at many levels, not only in the classrooms. Some modern dictionaries define civics simply as a branch of political science dealing with citizenship. However, if we go back to Aristotle and the best dictionaries, we find that civics is a broad body of knowledge dealing with the identification of different forms of government, the branches of government, political and electoral systems, balance of power in government, the rights and duties of citizens, ethics, and wealth distribution. In recent years the terms "politics" (the title of Aristotle's treatise) and "political science" have deviated far from their original meaning. Many of us today hold the very word politics in disdain. By contrast, Thomas Jefferson, when he wrote the Declaration of Independence, relied heavily on political philosophers, such as Aristotle, John Locke, and Jean-Jacques Rousseau for their essential wisdom and judgment. Therefore, I prefer to use the term "political philosophy" instead of political science.

After the Constitution High dedication, I began to ruminate. It did not seem to me a coincidence that civics disappeared during the same post-1980 period in which America suffered from an escalating series of institutional failures accompanied by gross corruption, malfeasance (wrongdoing), avarice in the people who possessed the most, and a new wave of demagoguery more deadly than the McCarthyism of the

1950's. My initial thought was to research the fundamental principles of civics applicable to a democratic republic by reading the original sources and compare them to the performance of the republic across a wide spectrum. Instead of writing another story of appalling scandals and malfeasance, I would do what Americans have most difficulty doing—I would connect the dots represented by these events and dig deeply to uncover the root causes of the systemic disease from which America appears to be suffering. I suspected I would find that our republic is no longer either a democracy or a republic and that it has degraded more or less along classical lines into a mix of despotism, oligarchy, and plutocracy, as these terms are defined here.

I visualized America as a very sick patient suffering from a systemic disease that has been progressive since the first outbreak in the early 1980's: The Savings & Loan Crisis. As subsequent outbreaks grew more severe, the infection spread precisely as Theodore Roosevelt maintained a century ago, through private corporations, regulatory agencies, Congress, the White House, the news media, and political parties. It was clear that America had received only *palliative* care from Congress. Palliative care only soothes a patient; it does not heal. It is unethical to apply palliative care when the patient has the potential to recover through a variety of treatment options. This is certainly true of America. Of course, the status quo of congressmen, politicians, demagogues, and business moguls would have to be changed.

I set some rules for myself. I would shun secondary sources in my research and concentrate on the original, authentic writings wherever possible in order to prevent false ideologies from creeping in. Author Susan Jacoby has described the decay of journalism into "infotainment" and the thirst for notoriety, fast profits, and superficial sound-bite entertainment. Her seminal book is titled *The Age of American Unreason.*[1]

I would commence by taking a patient history of America, as any good internist would do. This history would produce an authentic redefinition of the essence of America. I would examine prior episodes of good health and bad in order to determine America's inherent strengths and weaknesses. It makes no sense to fool ourselves by placing blame on a symptom of disease instead of the root cause; many of the accounts of accumulating failures in America in the last two or three decades focus on sensational eruptions or symptoms of a much larger and deeper systemic disease that people dare not or want not to uncover.

I decided to choose the period 1969–79 as the prototype of America's extraordinary resilience in the face of crises. Again, that period is most remembered for the sensational crises that occurred, and not for the high functioning of the republic in overcoming them and forging ahead with the civil rights and environmental laws that were models for the entire world. It is a matter of perspective. If James Madison had been alive then, he would have been fascinated by how the different branches of government and the people in them really did save the republic from downfall just as he had hoped. Also, this is the period I know best because 1 was in the U.S. Justice Department in Washington, D.C., legally representing the federal government and personally involved with all three branches of government.

This book is not intended to be a textbook. I write it for the general reader and to serve as supplemental reading in courses on American history, civics, democracy reform, and environmental policy, and for use in democracy-reform centers, of which America has many. I sifted through the treatises, Founders' archives, letters, journals, and newspaper archives to find the materials most relevant, enlightening, and interesting for our diagnosis and treatment of the systemic disease. Some of the stories and insights are good enough to stand on their own. The original words are often too magnificent and compelling not to be quoted. But the diagnosis and treatment cannot be given without also drawing the connections and parallels between then and now. The conclusions in the book are fortified by the remarkable overlap between these nuggets of wisdom extending back to Aristotle. Twenty-first century Americans have become prisoners of the flimsiest bursts of infotainment that replace the deep-probing journalism of the 1950's, 60's, and 70's. Unless we accept this truth and unite in a popular movement of democracy reform with the clear vision and vigor of the 1970's, the patient will sink further and further from a state of health and civic functionality.

We have much to gain by hastening to retrace our steps to find our future, as Jefferson urged in his First Inaugural. That is the only way out of civic breakdown.

To those who say I have cast too wide a net for any book by crossing over disciplines, centuries, and even millennia, I reply that wisdom has no bounds and the best of it emerges when one has lived long, read and discoursed widely, and maintained a generous, open mind, as Benjamin Franklin, for example, had done by the age of eighty-one, when he was senior delegate at the Constitutional Convention.

Finally, I opted not to shape the book chapters explicitly around principles of civics, root causes of disease, and remedies, as a textbook writer might do, but rather, to elicit these inanimate ideas from great people and great events portrayed vividly. We relate better to human beings and actual experiences. There is more life and energy in this approach. Of course, there is no limit to the number of pages that could be filled with observations on this subject, and Americans already have far too many distractions. Therefore, I have strived for brevity. This is in accord with my last chapter titled "Following Franklin." Franklin was beloved and admired for his ability to pierce through to the heart of the matter and, in few words, show the way with wit and wisdom. He remains our model.

Bradford F. Whitman
May 2016

---

[1] Susan Jacoby, *The Age of American Unreason* (New York: Pantheon, 2008).

Key Terms and Phrases

Articles of Association (1774) and Articles of Confederation and Perpetual Union (1777)—The two successive documents adopted by the Continental Congress in an attempt to formalize a legal association among the thirteen colonies/states during the Revolution. The Articles of Association were of no real significance for the Revolution; they provided for non-importation of British goods and an adherence to Puritanical or Quaker ways. The Articles of Confederation and Perpetual Union established the name "United States of America" and created a "firm league of friendship" among the states, but again, they created no central government. A "Committee of the States" requisitioned men and supplies from the states for General Washington, but compliance was spotty.

Bill of Rights (1791)—The first ten amendments to the United States Constitution that established the rights of individual citizens. George Mason, a brilliant young Virginia delegate to the 1787 Constitutional Convention, declined to sign the Constitution because the delegates, at the end of a long, hot summer in Philadelphia, deferred consideration of his bill of rights.

Civics—The body of knowledge originating from Aristotle's treatises circa 350 BC that included the strengths and weaknesses of different forms of government, political and electoral systems, balance of power, citizens' rights and duties, distribution of wealth, and ethics.

First and Second Continental Congresses—The provisional legislative government of the thirteen states before and during the Revolution. The members were appointed by the state legislatures for terms equal to three years in any six consecutive years; the members had to travel by horse to meet in Philadelphia on the appointed dates. The Continental Congress provided a forum for the delegates to meet and discuss the measures to be taken in response to England's oppressions, e.g., the signing of the Declaration of Independence, and to solidify the Revolution.

Congress—The legislature of the United States created by Article I of the United States Constitution and consisting of two houses: The House of Representatives (currently 435 members proportionately elected by the people of the respective states from Congressional districts to serve for two-year terms) and the Senate (100 members elected by the people, two per state for six-year terms).

Conservative and Neoconservative—The dictionary defines "conservative" as having a tendency to save and preserve something of value that exists. Theodore Roosevelt, circa 1912, commented on the appearance of a *new political faction* calling itself "the Conservatives." The faction was composed largely of businessmen, who, Roosevelt observed, seemed more interested in conserving their own status and wealth than in any fundamental principles of America. Senator Barry Goldwater in 1964 established a Conservative Party "to the right" of the Republicans. This faction, as it developed in succeeding years and ultimately became labelled the "Neoconservatives" in the 1980's, advocated a diminished federal government (except for seemingly unlimited spending for war-making), perennial restraints on federal regulation of private industry and domestic programs, and provisions to benefit special-interest groups and "moneyed factions."

Constitution—The United States Constitution written by delegates to the "Federal Convention" (the Constitutional Convention) in Philadelphia in 1787. It was later ratified by the states. The Constitution is the supreme law of the land; it establishes the powers and duties of the three branches of government: legislative, executive, and judicial.

Demagoguery—"Demagoguery" is derived from two Greek roots that mean "the people" (as in "democracy") and "to lead," i.e., leading the people. In this case, the "leading" of the people is not beneficial to the people; it is for the purpose of the demagogue's own personal and political gains. A demagogue is a political or other type of leader who exploits the ignorance of the audience with false or exaggerated claims and promises, false allegations, fear-mongering, and often divisive appeals to prejudice against races, ethnic groups, and social classes. The tools of the demagogue are his words—his rhetoric.

Democracy—The form of government in which the people retain ultimate power. Aristotle distinguished between "pure democracy" in which the people themselves take control of government, and "representative democracy" in which the people retain ultimate governmental power but entrust the acts of government to elected representatives.

Democratic Republic—A representative democracy, such as that formed by the Founders.

Despotism—A government or political system in which an individual or a few individuals exercise absolute power; it is the rule of man, not the law.

Fiefdom—Originally, the feudal estate of an overlord in the Middle Ages that was in the form of a tract of land or a title or office over which he exercised complete control and from which he received goods, income, or service through his vassals. Theodore Roosevelt and others have used the feudal relationship as a metaphor to describe the huge wealth and property gaps that developed between classes in America with the "robber barons" at the beginning of the twentieth century and again post-1980.

Filibuster—The making of prolonged speeches and introduction of irrelevant material for the purpose of delaying legislative action on a pending bill or resolution.

Founders—The term "Founders" is used here to refer to the individuals who contributed to the actual founding of the United States through their words and actions in the late eighteenth century. Some of America's great patriots were not Founders because they were not involved in the actual founding of the republic, although they made the Founding possible by winning the Revolution.

Infotainment—A word borrowed from Susan Jacoby's book, *The Age of American Unreason*[1], that means the use of information to entertain, not enlighten. Infotainment is the post-1970's metamorphosis of journalism. It is a twenty-four-hour-a-day industry that sacrifices reason and responsibility to sensationalism and sales.

Hubris—A word derived from the Greek that means a mixture of overbearing pride, ambition, and arrogance that blinds a person to the truth—and typically leads to disaster for the hubristic individual and the victims. The term has its origins in Greek and Shakespearean tragedy.

Liberty—Liberty means freedom. For the Founders and the men of the eighteenth century Age of Reason or Enlightenment, it meant civil liberty, as described in Chapter 1.

Malfeasance—An act of wrongdoing, especially by a person holding a public or private office, under color of the authority of his office. The metaphor *avalanche of malfeasance* is used in this book to describe the outbreak of lawlessness and wrongdoing in business and finance that commenced with the Savings & Loan Crisis of the early 1980's, gathered power, size, and speed as the years progressed, and obliterated giant U.S. banks and corporations—and the investments of millions of Americans. The avalanche changes shape and form and continues to this day.

Narcissism—A word derived from the classical myth of Narcissus who fell in love with his *own* image and died of unrequited love. Narcissism means blind self-absorption.

NGO—Non-governmental organization, usually a nonprofit group.

Nonfeasance—The failure to perform official duties.

Oligarchy—Rule by the few.

Plutocracy—Rule by the wealthy.

Plutocrat—A person with power or influence associated with wealth.

Popular Sovereignty—A doctrine in political philosophy that sovereignty [the power to rule] is vested in the people as a whole rather than in a particular individual, faction, or entity. The doctrine has its roots in the work of the seventeenth century English political philosopher, John Locke, who influenced the Founders. The term is somewhat misleading when used in regard to a democratic republic because the people do not rule directly, but through elected representatives; however, the people retain ultimate political power to "censor their governors" (Jefferson's phrase).

Social Contract—An agreement among individuals by which an organized society is brought into being and which serves to regulate the relationships of the members of a society with each other and with the government. Jean-Jacques Rousseau was the leading eighteenth-century proponent of social contract theory. It is explained in Chapter 1.

Systemic Disease—A spreading disease of the entire body or system, as opposed to a disease that afflicts only a part of the body. The term is applied here as a metaphor for the progressive corruption and dysfunction of America's government, private industry, and news media. Systemic diseases cannot be halted by treating individual parts of the body; a comprehensive treatment regimen is needed.

Top Decile—The term used herein refers to the top 10% of taxpayers ranked by annual income reported to the Internal Revenue Service.

Top Percentile—The term used herein refers to the top 1% of taxpayers ranked by annual income reported to the Internal Revenue Service.

Universal Service—Mandatory public service for all citizens between certain ages, e.g., 18-24, extending for a year or two, with the purpose of achieving broad public good, making citizens aware of the circumstances and needs of fellow citizens who are removed from them by socioeconomic class, ethnicity, geography, or age. Universal service has been used in many countries to promote understanding and empathy among the people and a sense of mutual respect, and to strengthen the common bonds to country and to founding principles. There is a social benefit from the service provided.

---

[1] Susan Jacoby, *The Age of American Unreason* (New York: Pantheon, 2008).

Introduction

"Let us then fellow-citizens unite with one heart and one mind. Let us restore to social intercourse that harmony and affection without which liberty and even life itself are but dreary things. And let us reflect that, having banished from our land that religious intolerance under which mankind so long bled and suffered, we have yet gained little if we countenance a political intolerance as despotic, as wicked, and as capable of as bitter and bloody persecutions... The wisdom of our sages and blood of our heroes have been devoted to their [the fundamental principles'] attainment. They should be the creed of our political faith, the text of civic instruction, the touchstone by which we try the services of those we trust; should we wander from them in moments of error or alarm, let us hasten to retrace our steps and to regain the road which alone leads to peace, liberty, and safety."

–Thomas Jefferson, First Inaugural Address, March 4, 1801

"The people are the only censors of their governors: and even their errors will tend to keep these [the governors] to the true principles of their institution. To punish these errors too severely would be to suppress the only safeguard of the public liberty. The way to prevent these irregular interpositions of the people is to give them full information of their affairs thro' the channel of the public papers, and to contrive that those papers should penetrate the whole mass of the people. The basis of our governments being the opinion of the people, the very first object should be to keep that right... Cherish therefore the spirit of the people, and keep alive their attention. Do not be too severe upon their errors, but reclaim them by enlightening them. If once they become inattentive to public affairs, you & I, & Congress & Assemblies, judges & governors shall all become wolves."

–Thomas Jefferson, "To Edward Carrington, Paris, January 16, 1787"[1]

---

[1] Thomas Jefferson, "From Thomas Jefferson to Edward Carrington, 16 January 1787," National Archives: Founders Online; http://founders.archives.gov/documents/Jefferson/01-11-02-0047 ("Carrington letter").

Chapter 1

Life, Liberty, and the Pursuit of Happiness

"...We hold these truths to be self-evident, that all men are created equal, that they are endowed by their Creator with certain unalienable Rights, that among these are Life, Liberty, and the pursuit of Happiness... That whenever any Form of Government becomes destructive of these ends, it is the Right of the People to alter or abolish it."
–Thomas Jefferson, Declaration of Independence (July 4, 1776)[1]

"What man loses by the social contract is his natural liberty and an unlimited right to everything he tries to get and succeeds in getting; what he gains is civil liberty."
–Jean-Jacques Rousseau (1762)[2]

In the Declaration of Independence Thomas Jefferson declared three inalienable[3] rights of mankind. These rights are given to us as human beings; they cannot be taken from us, and we cannot "alienate" them by any intentional or coerced act or deed. They are at the top of the pyramid of all political, social, and legal rights and benefits that flow from being part of a "social contract" for governance. "[W]henever any Form of Government becomes destructive of these ends, it is the Right of the People to alter or to abolish it," Jefferson continued.[4] The rights to liberty and happiness, despite centuries of comment, are poorly understood today and have become some of the worst victims of demagoguery. They cannot be fully known without retracing the steps back to America's Founding and the political philosophy of Jean-Jacques Rousseau, who was a virtual contemporary of Jefferson in the Age of Enlightenment. The consequences of misinterpretation of the inalienable right to liberty have been grave.

Teaching or reading the Declaration of Independence, the first of two documents that define the essence of America, without examining the critical background and context of Jefferson's writing is a setup for a lot of self-serving misinterpretation. Furthermore, the statement of the inalienable rights is closely followed by the fundamental principle

3

originally espoused by John Locke that whenever any form of government becomes destructive of these ends, it is the right of the people to alter or abolish it. Obviously, in 1776 Jefferson was applying this principle to the King and Parliament, but it applies with equal force to our *own* branches of government. The obsessive attention given today to politicians by the infotainment industry has taken our eyes off the main goal of American democracy—that we the People must all become educated, informed, and involved, as full citizens, in the censoring of our governors, as Jefferson said in the Carrington letter quoted above.

The background and context for the Declaration and the U.S. Constitution include the following items: the writings of classical political philosophers such as Aristotle; the history of failed republics, e.g., Rome; the language of several state constitutions previously written by some of the Founders, e.g., Virginia's (by George Mason), Pennsylvania's (by Franklin), and Massachusetts' (by John Adams); some startlingly relevant correspondence from the Founders as well as speeches and essays and the more formal *Federalist Papers* written to explain and promote the ratification of the Constitution.[5] This is not a textbook or a PhD dissertation; the best way to present these materials is to distill them down to items of particular relevance to our condition today. The political philosophers, the Founders, and their greatest political descendants had astounding foresight and understanding of human nature, and social and political entities.

The scope of our inquiry is *civics*. One reason why a society as saturated with communication as America is cannot heal itself—or even acknowledge and confront the disease—is that the information communicated is tailored to fit people who want immediate gratification. As we will see, that type of information provides neither gratification nor the enlightenment necessary to reverse America's slide. Civics is the body of knowledge originally assembled by Aristotle circa 350 BC in Greece. It includes the identification of different forms of government, the branches of government, political and electoral systems, the balance of power in government and society, the rights and duties of citizens, the distribution of wealth, and ethics. These may seem topics of academic interest only; as the Declaration proclaims, quite the reverse is true. Our ability to attain the ultimate goals of life, liberty, happiness, and, as George Washington said, "a great and happy people" depends directly on the people learning and applying civics.

The first step in taking America's patient history is to place ourselves in the eighteenth century, the Age of Enlightenment, or Reason, when the Declaration and Constitution were written. The Founders—Jefferson, Franklin, and Adams in particular—lived for a while in the center of the European Enlightenment, in Paris. The Enlightenment movement was not dissimilar to movements that later occurred in this country, such as the civil rights and environmental movements in the 1970's that are the subject of later chapters. The Founders embraced enthusiastically the pursuit of arts and sciences, knowledge, and philosophy.

Jefferson mentioned "the elementary books of public right, as Aristotle, Cicero, Locke, Sidney, ETC."[6] (We devote a separate chapter to Aristotle. Political philosopher John Locke in England in the seventeenth century and Jean-Jacques Rousseau in France in the eighteenth century were major influences on Jefferson.) In the same letter Jefferson referred to his Declaration as an "expression of the American mind."[7] Establishing a "new republic" was the Founders' chance to put into effect the democratic principles they had learned and to free the colonists from the hierarchical oppressions that prevailed in Europe. Thus, the Founders and their constituents developed their own set of fundamental principles that were neither clones of classical ideas nor rebellious breakouts. Author Catherine Drinker Bowen has written of the *miracle* of the 1787 Constitutional Convention.[8] One of the other "miracles" was that the Founders, separated by great distances and settings (urban versus rural), held fast to a common set of ethical and civic principles because they were right and good and timely; they did not need modern means of communication to produce the greatest written constitution for any democracy in history.

America had printing presses in 1776, but America did not have book publishers. Thus, Americans read newspapers, but lacked direct access to the wisdom of the ages in books. Jefferson and Franklin came to the rescue. They busied themselves with importing the classics and making them available to their colleagues. Jefferson was a compulsive bibliophile; he purchased books from Europe in astounding numbers—

spending far more than a reasonable portion of his liquid assets. His Monticello, Virginia, library was vast, and the Library of Congress possesses much of it now.[9] Franklin established the Library Company of Philadelphia as a subscription lending library. The National Constitution Center in Philadelphia now maintains a small alcove of facsimiles of works to which the Founders had access when they wrote the Constitution. The classics we have noted are in that alcove.

Jefferson knew the French language, liked France, and undoubtedly read and relied on Rousseau's *Social Contract*. Rousseau's main work was published in 1762. An indication of Rousseau's position in America was that the brilliant Philadelphian Nicholas Biddle, who championed the cause of a national bank of the United States and, among other things, transcribed the notes of the Lewis and Clark Expedition at Jefferson's request, acquired a copy of *The Social Contract* in 1803.[10] The treatises of Aristotle and Locke were standard teaching texts.

Jefferson had been tutored by George Wythe, a Virginian, an expert in the law, a man of virtue and patriotism, a proponent of the "natural and equal rights of man", and a master of Greek and Latin. Jefferson described Wythe as the "Cato [great Roman orator and philosopher] of his country, without the *avarice* [greed] of the Roman."[11]

One of the Founders' earliest writings on the subject of governance was a private, personal rumination by the Harvard-educated John Adams in Massachusetts, and it represents one part of the context of the Founding, albeit not a major one. The Adams-Jefferson relationship was epic in many ways, with great highs and lows. Before we look at Adams' rough essay, we should see how he regarded the choice of Jefferson to write the Declaration of Independence when he (Adams) was appointed by the Congress to the drafting committee of five along with Jefferson and Franklin. Adams said that he declined Jefferson's suggestion that he, Adams, should draft the Declaration partly because he had been such a strong and "obnoxious" advocate for independence that he thought any draft he produced would draw excessive scrutiny and criticism from others in the Congress.[12] Adams also said that even if there were no other reason to choose Jefferson, the "elegance" of Jefferson's pen—and "none at all of mine own"—should be sufficient to carry the day.[13]

Adams believed strongly in the *rule of law*. The distinguishing characteristic of a democratic republic is the rule of law, not men. Adams put his beliefs to the test when he ably defended at trial the British soldiers charged with the "Boston Massacre" (not a massacre at all, but a bungled reaction to ugly provocation by some colonists). In April 1776 Adams wrote *"Thoughts on Government."*[14] He declared first that the happiness of society is the goal of government.[15] At first glance this proposition seems rather obvious or trite—but then who among us today, informed and objective, could maintain that the government of the United States during the last three decades has attained, or even steadfastly pursued, the happiness of society as a whole?

It is gratifying that Adams and Jefferson both placed the pursuit of happiness at the top of the pyramid, not the building of an empire or the acquisition of enormous wealth and power. Julius Caesars they were not.

Adams then stated that the form of government that *promotes virtue* (Aristotle's signature word) is the one that promotes the general happiness of society. We will be discussing "virtue" at some length because most of the Founders realized that if government is to be conducted through elected representatives, the representatives must possess virtue. They would never be free of personal ambition and desires, but they would have to be able to raise virtue and country above self while seeking and holding public office. Adams defined a republic as an "empire of laws, not men," a good way of distinguishing the failed republics from the healthy ones.

There is substantial overlap between the Founders' fundamental principles and the Judeo-Christian tenets of faith (many of which are also tenets of faith of other great religions of the world). This overlap strengthens and reinforces the principles, but we should make no mistake here. The principles are ones of *civics*, not religion. They were developed by Aristotle circa 350 BC in Athens. Christianity played no role in their development. The principles are at the core of good democratic government.

Adams recognized the need for checks and balances in government to prevent ambition, greed, and corruption from destroying the system.

James Madison is famous for developing this concept at the Constitutional Convention and for negotiating among the delegates the terms of a written constitution based on checks and balances. The concept was not new to civics. Aristotle understood that the legislative branch was inherently the most powerful and most likely to abuse its power. It had to be checked. Adams did not hold back when describing legislators. He said they should be turned out of office at regular intervals to teach them the "great political virtues of humility, patience, and moderation without which every man becomes a ravenous beast of prey."[16] No era has more decisively proved the truth of this principle than the present.

Adams thought that enough friction would develop between the legislature and the executive to warrant the creation of a council to mediate disputes—an interesting idea. In the two-party system we have today, the friction has evolved into open hostility and political revenge, as George Washington described. Having more political parties would probably decrease the intense antagonism. Having a body of representatives serve as a mediator on Capitol Hill might function similarly to assigning mediators to resolve legal disputes in court. When ego and empowerment issues are handled first, there is space for some reason to enter in. The players would have to agree to put aside their grandstanding before the press.

Adams passionately supported the enactment of laws for the liberal education of youth. He said that "to a humane and generous mind no expense for this purpose [public education] would be thought extravagant." We will return to this subject in a later chapter.

Finally, Adams, in his draft of the Massachusetts Constitution in 1780 said it was absolutely necessary to return frequently to these fundamental principles. There were precisely parallel provisions in the original Virginia and Pennsylvania Constitutions (authored respectively by Jefferson and Franklin) that required frequent return to the fundamental principles.[17] The failure of modern American public and private leaders to take time out and reconsider fundamental principles of law, ethics, and the social contract jumps out as one of the greatest betrayals of the Founders. The principle manifested itself in many ways. When Adams became vice president, he demanded that Congress commence every new session with a reading aloud of George

Washington's Farewell Address, an excellent way of retracing steps. The practice continued for years, but Congress discontinued the readings just when they were of most importance. We will return to that address later.

Thomas Jefferson did not have a lot of time to draft the Declaration of Independence. He set to work in a private house, now known as the Declaration House, in Philadelphia, and he completed his draft and various rounds of revisions in approximately three weeks. His close friend, the young scholar George Mason (in his twenties), had just completed the Commonwealth of Virginia's Declaration of Rights[18]; it was approved on June 12, 1776. Jefferson had Mason's work in front of him. Before we compare Mason's Declaration to Jefferson's Declaration, we should look at the seminal work of John Locke, the English philosopher who, for the first time in 1690, rejected the doctrine of the divine right of kings and declared that the origin of all political power lay in the people. The people had the ultimate authority to correct abuses of government.

"Popular sovereignty" is not the best choice of words to summarize Locke's doctrine because it suggests that the people themselves actually govern the republic from day to day. Our democracy is a representative democracy. Nevertheless, no better phrase exists, and we will use it with that qualification.

Locke stated in his Second Treatise of Government:

But if they [the people] have set limits to the duration of their legislative [sic], or else when by miscarriages of those in authority, it [supreme power] is forfeited, upon the forfeiture [of the legislature's right to govern], or at the determination of the time set, it [the power] reverts to the society, and the people have the right to act as supreme, and continue the legislative in themselves; or erect a new form, or under the old form place it in new hands as they think good.[19]

Social and political order until that moment had been strictly hierarchical—from the king on down through noblemen and property-holders to the disempowered mass of humanity. By contrast, Locke held that ultimate political power resides not in a king or his nobles, but in the people. In his treatise, Locke also introduced the concept of government as a social contract formed by the people that requires them, for their own good and collective well-being, to abandon the unrestrained liberty that exists in the state of nature. Rousseau developed this idea.

It is little known that Roger Williams, the dissenting Puritan who founded Rhode Island, actually preceded Locke in publishing the principle of popular sovereignty and the right to freedom of religion. His rough mini-treatise was published in London in July 1644; it stated there that the foundation of civil power—sovereignty—lies in the people.[20]

For the reasons expressed, Jefferson was bound to be affected by Jean-Jacques Rousseau's publication in 1762 of *The Social Contract or Principles of Political Right.*[21] Rousseau concluded that when man was living in a pure state of nature, he learned that he could not survive— and certainly not prosper—without anyone but himself upon whom to rely. As a solitary individual, man was vulnerable and weak. (I use the term *man* throughout in a genderless sense to mean *mankind.*) Therefore, man decided to depart from the pure state of nature, to enter into a social contract with other men, and, in the process, to forfeit or surrender the *unrestrained* freedom and vulnerability that exist in the pure state. The benefits of the social contract far outweighed the loss of total, unrestrained freedom. Rousseau expressed this trade-off as follows:

"What a man loses by the social contract is his natural liberty and an unlimited right to everything he tries to get and succeeds in getting; what he gains is civil liberty and the proprietorship of all he possesses."[22]

This single sentence crystalizes the meaning of civil liberty in the Age of Enlightenment—for Jefferson and the Founders as well as Rousseau. The original, authentic essence of America hangs on this principle: man loses the unlimited right to everything he tries to get and succeeds in getting. A society where people follow the opposite course and accept no restraints on greed and ambition is alien to the American republic. It is one where people become ravenous beasts of prey, and the descent into despotism, oligarchy, and plutocracy is inevitable.

George Washington, at the end of his second term as president, expressed the same thought regarding the way to achieve liberty in society. He said: "Liberty itself will find in such a government [a vigorous federal government], with powers properly distributed and adjusted, its surest guardian."[23]

Washington, who was deeply devoted to the long-term success of the new republic, predicted (like Madison) that America's greatest threat would come from within, from individuals and factions seeking their own gain. Therefore, a vigorous federal government with its powers "properly distributed and adjusted" was the surest guardian of liberty.

Rousseau took the analysis one step further. He equated civil liberty with moral liberty "which alone makes [man] truly master of himself, for the mere impulse of appetite is slavery."[24] A life driven by personal appetite, by avarice, is a life deprived of liberty. A social contract is similar to a legal contract; there are mutual benefits and obligations on both sides. It is always a two-way street—and there are always restraints, civic commitments, and sacrifices. From this analysis it is clear that the ideology of so-called Neoconservatives today is not conservative at all; in fact, it is the antithesis of the original concept of civil liberty.

George Mason was the youngest delegate to the Constitutional Convention in 1787. Jefferson called him "the wisest man of his generation."[25] Nevertheless, with youth often comes an impetuous nature, and it is sad to see that Mason became so insistent on extending the Constitutional Convention to adopt his Bill of Rights that he refused to approve the Constitution without it; the Bill of Rights came in four years later. Mason also campaigned against ratification of the Constitution on the same ground and lost that too.

In any event, Mason, in his June 12, 1776 Virginia Declaration of Rights, had recited a *fourth* inalienable right: "the means of acquiring and possessing property."[26] Under the circumstances, it was impossible for Jefferson to have overlooked Mason's fourth right of property. It conflicted with Rousseau's articulation of civil liberty that we have just discussed. Jefferson made a deliberate decision to place life, liberty, and the pursuit of happiness at the top of the pyramid—and put property aside. Jefferson was often praised by Adams and others for having a good ear for the sentiment of the people, and his decision in this instance was true to himself, to the people, and to the Continental Congress that appointed him.

Jefferson's Declaration was approved with only formalistic edits by the other four committee members and one major edit by Congress to strike out his impassioned anti-slave-trade provision (rarely mentioned by modern revisionists).

George Mason himself made it clear that he was strongly opposed to the *disproportionate* holding of riches by any individual or faction. Mason believed that an excess of wealth or property—"luxury" in his words—undermined the civic virtue on which republican governments depended.[27] By defending the right to acquire property, Mason was merely repudiating the class system in Europe, not inviting a society that opened its doors to unrestrained getting and spending. Rousseau wrote that "the social state is advantageous to men when all have something and none too much."[28] It was this egalitarian view of wealth that prevailed among the Founders as we shall see at the Constitutional Convention.

With regard to "happiness," there has been a recent surge in interest on the part of psychologists and neuroscientists, and they have filled some of the gaps. This new field is generally referred to as "positive psychology." The books written on this subject in the last ten years are impressive, both in their number and their diversity. A good primer on happiness is the Public Broadcasting Service television program: *The Science of Happiness, Life (Part 2)*.[29] One of the speakers, a Harvard professor, Tal Ben-Shahar, has written some of the leading texts.[30] Studies have been conducted in a wide variety of societies, cultures, and countries; the findings have been impressively uniform. First, happiness is distinguished from the state of temporary euphoria that we know as a giddy high. Happiness is long-term contentment.

Second, people who have excessive material expectations (of money, goods, and possessions) rarely achieve contentment. This finding is age-old, but the use of scientific studies to prove it is new. The Founders did not need scientific studies to know this truth. Happiness researchers found that contentment is closely associated with virtue, just as Aristotle and the Founders believed. The aspects of virtue mentioned were a sense of personal gratitude, felt and expressed;

an attitude and practice of giving to others; and a sense of forgiveness for the past (especially for one's own actions and beliefs). The researchers also identified, as inducers of happiness, a routine of regular aerobic exercise, focusing one's attention on the here and now, and cultivating friendships.

Finally, we will take a look at the pledge by the signers at the end of the Declaration of Independence. In 1776 the war was going poorly for the colonists. Until General Washington crossed the Delaware River and won the Battle of Trenton, his army had been in retreat. The signers' pledge at the end of the Declaration was a bold move. There was a good chance the colonial army would lose the war, and if that happened, the signers of the Declaration would have been high on King George's list of traitors to be hanged.

The signers pledged to fight for independence with their *"lives, fortunes, and sacred honor."* A person could give no more than that. The signers took their pledge seriously, as we will see, and it stood then—and forever—as a hallmark of good American citizenship.

---

[1] The Declaration was adopted by the Second Continental Congress on July 4, 1776, read aloud on July 8, and printed in Philadelphia. One of the best online repositories of eighteenth century American writings is Yale Law School's Avalon Project. Yale Law School, Lillian Goldman Law Library, *The Avalon Project—Documents in Law, History and Diplomacy* (hereafter *"Avalon"*); http://avalon.law.yale.edu/18th_century/fed10.asp. All of the documents I cite from Avalon are in the "18ᵗʰ Century" documents collection.

[2] Jean-Jacques Rousseau, *The Social Contract or Principles of Political Right* (1762), reproduced in *Everyman's Library—Philosophy and Theology, The Social Contract & Discourses by Jean-Jacques Rousseau*, tr. G.D.H. Cole, ed. Ernest Rhys, (New York: Dutton, 1920), Book I, Ch. 8, 19. Books.google.com.

[3] Jefferson originally used "inalienable," a more sonorous and correct spelling of this legal word. It was unfortunately edited to "unalicnable." Jefferson's good ear prevailed in the end, and the modern usage by lawyers is "inalienable."

[4] Declaration, *Avalon.*

[5] These essays appeared first as newspaper letters signed "Publius." They were then collected in a volume to explain the provisions of the Constitution and promote its ratification by the thirteen states. I relied on one paper copy, *The Federalist Papers* (New York: Mentor Books, 1961), and the online reproduction in *Avalon.*

[6] Jefferson, "From Thomas Jefferson to Henry Lee, 8 May 1825," National Archives, Founders Online; http://founders.archives.gov /documents.

[7] Id.

[8] Catherine Drinker Bowen, *Miracle at Philadelphia—The Story of the Constitutional Convention* (New York: Back Bay Books/Little Brown, 1986).

[9] Thomas Jefferson Portal Online Library Catalog; http://tjportal .monticello.org.

[10] Personal Communication from Connie S. Griffith Houchins, Executive Director, The Andalusia Foundation, www.andalusiapa.org, forwarding a facsimile of Nicholas Biddle's handwritten "List of My Books—September 9, 1803" received in part from Dr. Enoch Edwards, physician to George Washington.

[11] Thomas Jefferson, *The Writings of Thomas Jefferson–Memoir, Correspondence and Miscellanies,* ed. Thomas Jefferson Randolph (Charlottesville: F. Carr & Co., 1829), Vol. 1, 93 (my emphasis).

[12] John Adams, *Autobiography,* collected by the Massachusetts Historical Society in *Adams Family Papers, An Electronic Archive,* part 1, through 1776, sheet 24 of 53, April–August 1776; http://www.masshist.org.

[13] Id.

[14] John Adams, *Thoughts on Government* (April 1776), collected in *The Adams Papers,* The Constitution Society, 4:86–93; http://www.constitution .org/jadams/thoughts.htm (hereafter, *Thoughts*).

[15] *Thoughts*.

[16] *Thoughts*.

[17] *Constitution of Massachusetts*, Art. XVIII (1780), reproduced by the National Humanities Institute, Center for Constitutional Studies. www.nhinet.org/ccs/docs/ma-1780. *The Virginia Declaration of Rights*, Art. 15 (June 12, 1776), reproduced in *Avalon*. See also, *The Charters of Freedom,* reproduced in www.archives.gov/exhibits/charters/. Pennsylvania Constitution, Art. XIV (1776), reproduced in *Avalon*.

[18] National Endowment for the Humanities, "George Mason and the Virginia Declaration," http://edsitement.neh.gov.

[19] John Locke, *The Second Treatise of Civil Government* (1690), collected in *Project Gutenberg EBook of Second Treatise of Government by John Locke,* Book XIX, Sec. 243, 28 July 2010, rev. 6 January 2014 (my emphasis). http://projectgutenberg.org. See also, The Constitution Society. http://www.constitution.org/jl/2n.

[20] Roger Williams, *The Bloody Tenent, of Persecution, for Cause of Conscience, discussed in A Conference between Truth and Peace* (London: 1644).

[21] Jean-Jacques Rousseau, *The Social Contract or Principles of Political Right* (1762), tr. G.D.H. Cole, The Constitution Society. http://www.constitution .org. See also, Ernest Rhys ed., *Everyman's Library, Philosophy & Theology—The Social Contract & Discourses* (New York: Dutton, 1920).

[22] *The Social Contract,* I, Sec. 8.

[23] George Washington, *The Farewell Address* (1796), reproduced in *Avalon.*

[24] Id.

[25] Editor's Introduction to The Virginia Declaration of Rights. www.nationalcenter.org/VirginiaDeclaration.html. Comment also contained in Thomas Jefferson, *The Writings of Thomas Jefferson: Autobiography with Appendix,* ed. H.A. Washington (New York: John C. Riker, 1853), collected in Google Books. http://books.google.com.

[26] George Mason, *The Virginia Declaration of Rights*, Art. I. *Avalon.*

[27] Jeff Broadwater, *Why George Mason Matters.* History News Network. http://www.historynewsnetwork.org/article/47847.

[28] The Social Contract, I, Sec. 9, n. 5.

[29] PBS (Robert Lipsyte, Moderator). *The Science of Happiness. Life (Part 2).* http://www.pbs.org/lifepart2/watch/season-2/-science-happiness.

[30] Tal Ben-Shahar, *Happier: Learn the Secrets to Daily Joy and Lasting Fulfillment* (New York: McGraw-Hill, 2007).

Chapter 2

Aristotle and the Founders

"Thus it is manifest that *the best political community formed by citizens is formed by citizens of the middle class,* and that those states are likely to be well-administered in which the middle class is large for the addition of the middle class turns the scale, and prevents either of the extremes from being dominant. *Great then is the good fortune of a state in which the citizens have a moderate and sufficient property...* The mean condition of states is clearly best, for no other is free from faction, and where the middle class is large, there are least likely to be factions and dissensions... And *democracies are safer and more permanent than oligarchies,* because they have a middle class which is more numerous and has a greater share in the government."
—*Aristotle (350 BC)*

Aristotle was the father of western political philosophy. He wrote *Politics* in eight "books" (long chapters) circa 350 BC, among other treatises. Aristotle was an aristocratic intellectual whom I did not expect to embrace heartily a democratic republic formed by the middle class. He referred to it as "the *best* political community formed by citizens," and he analyzed it—and the other forms—from many different perspectives. *Politics* is exhaustive, sometimes inconsistent, and garrulous, but Jowett's translation is very readable, and Aristotle's wisdom and foresight are often astounding. It is superficial for anyone to teach the essence of America without including this incisive explanation of a democratic republic. Many times, as we will see, the Founders called for future generations to be instructed in these very principles so that they would be capable of managing a republic.

Aristotle was quick to tell us that this "best political community formed by citizens" is formed and maintained by the middle class. There have been many instances of American "leaders" betraying the Founders and their principles during the last thirty years, but none is more offensive than the building up of the rich and tearing down of the middle class. In Aristotle's view, the middle class tips the scale toward a successful republic. There must be a large and expanding middle class to prevent the extremes of poverty and deprivation at one end and affluence at the other from undermining the republic. Aristotle stated that the very rich tend to be focused on material goods, personal gain, and power; they tend to become plutocrats. The disadvantaged struggle to maintain a decent life and have less opportunity to educate and inform themselves and engage in civic affairs. These are generalizations, of course, but inescapable ones. The greatest long-term public good comes from a state in which the citizens have "a moderate and sufficient property," Aristotle said. Jean-Jacques Rousseau wrote almost identical words in the eighteenth century. At the Constitutional Convention the Founders voiced the same principle.

Aristotle believed that where there are great inequities in wealth distribution, dangerous factions and dissensions arise. When Aristotle said that the "mean [average] condition of states is clearly best," he was saying that a state prospers when it is well balanced, economically and socially. Aristotle commented that "the greatest crimes are caused by excess and not by necessity."[1] Interestingly, Benjamin Franklin uttered a similar comment at the Convention: "Some of the greatest rogues he [Franklin] was ever acquainted with were the richest rogues."[2] Proof of this point is set forth in the chapter on industry.

Aristotle insisted that wealth not be permitted to infect and influence the *selection of public representatives*. He wrote:

> The law which allows this abuse [the use of wealth to acquire public office] makes wealth of more account than virtue, and the whole state becomes avaricious... Those who have been at the expense of purchasing their places will be in the habit of repaying themselves.[3]

Aristotle sets up the dichotomy between greed and wealth on the one hand and virtue and good government on the other. One wonders how he could have foreseen the disastrous consequences of mingling private fortunes with public office. Greece had no mountain of drachmas to compare to the billions of dollars that have contaminated the political process in America.

Aristotle explained that pure democracy is government by the people directly, not through elected representatives. Neither Aristotle nor the Founders favored this form because it often leads to anarchy, dysfunction, and, at its extreme, a bloody reign of terror like that in France in the late eighteenth century. By contrast, in a representative democracy the people elect representatives to carry out government. It is the best compromise—but the citizens must be capable and willing to censor their governors.

Aristotle wrote that:

> No one will doubt that the legislator should direct his attention above all to the education of youth; for the neglect of education does harm to the constitution. The citizen should be moulded [through education] to suit the form of government under which he lives. For each government has a peculiar character which originally formed and continues to preserve it. The character of democracy creates democracy, and character of oligarchy creates oligarchy...[4]

The idea that neglecting the public education that shapes good citizens is an attack on the very foundation of the republic was easy for the Founders to grasp; it has completely eluded modern political leaders. Aristotle reminded legislators that their attention should be directed *above all* to the education of the youth that forms citizens. Aristotle expected permanent inhabitants to be citizens of the country and properly educated; slaves, however, existed then as they did for another two millennia, even in republics.

Aristotle stressed the teaching of liberal arts, the humanities, and civics. He mentions reading and writing, music and drawing, physical fitness, and the liberal arts.[5] Even in 350 BC Aristotle understood the proper role for vocational education. He said that "[t]o be always seeking after the useful does not become [is not becoming to or appropriate for] free and exalted souls."[6] It is no coincidence that the collapse of representative democracy in America has been paralleled by a collapse in the teaching of humanities, arts, and civics.

The words "demagogue" and "demagoguery" that are defined in the list of Key Terms and Phrases had their origin in Aristotle's writings. Aristotle said that where the laws are not supreme, demagogues spring up at the expense of democracy.[7]

Finally, Aristotle believed that ethics and politics cannot be separated. There must be virtue in politics. He characterized the state as an extension of the individual, which is consistent with the idea that the people retain ultimate political power. Therefore, it is natural and productive for us to regard the state and the political system as precious to us—like an organ or part of our body, an arm or a leg. This should be the norm. Decades of Neoconservative demagoguery have torn away at this fundamental principle. Aristotle identified the qualities that make up virtue. He named wisdom, loyalty to the constitution, excellent administrative ability, and a desire for justice.[8] Aristotle also said that virtue is intertwined with happiness, which is consistent with the modern scientific findings we discussed. George Washington in his First Inaugural Address said that there is "an indissoluble union between virtue and happiness."[9]

At the same time, Aristotle understood that man is not *innately* virtuous—at least not sufficiently virtuous. Virtue must be taught and learned. Virtue includes honesty and integrity, diligence, and self-restraint. Virtue is the opposite of narcissism and hubris. Aristotle was aggressive on this point. He denied that "any one of the citizens belongs to himself, for they all belong to the state, and are each of them a part of the state, and the care of each part is inseparable from the care of the whole."[10] The philosopher Rousseau embraced Aristotle's idea that a citizen cannot divorce himself from his government.

Aristotle's principles in large part became the Founder's principles. More than two thousand years of history have affirmed their wisdom. Those states that abandoned them have failed. Aristotle made clear that human beings cannot be expected to meet all these standards, but no society expecting or hoping to enjoy the great benefits of representative democracy should be shocked by the consequences of utter betrayal.

---

[1] *Politics*, Bk. II, Ch. 7, 1160.

[2] James Madison, *The Papers of James Madison and his Reports of Debates in the Federal Convention*, ed. Henry D. Gilpin (Washington, DC: Langtree & O'Sullivan, 1840), III, 1285 (hereafter "*Notes*"). I chose Gilpin's edition because it is comprehensive and closest in time to the event. See also, the online edition of the *Notes* in Avalon.

[3] *Politics,* Bk. II, Ch. 11, 1173.

[4] *Politics,* Bk. VIII, Ch. 1, 1305.

[5] *Politics,* Bk. VIII, Ch. 2, 1306.

[6] *Politics*, Bk. VIII, Ch. 3, 1308.

[7] *Politics*, Bk. IV, Ch. 4, 1212.

[8] *Politics,* Bk. V, Ch. 8, 1249.

[9] George Washington, "First Inaugural Address—April 30, 1789" collected in The Library of America, *American Speeches: The Revolution to the Civil War* (New York: Literary Classics of America, 2006).

[10] *Politics*, Bk. VIII, Ch. 1, 1305.

Chapter 3

Benjamin Franklin–Champion of the Middle Class

"I served with George Washington in the legislature of Virginia before the Revolution, and during it, with Dr. Franklin in Congress. I never heard either of them speak ten minutes at a time, nor to any but the main point which was to decide the question. They laid their shoulders to the great points, knowing that the little ones would follow of themselves."

—Thomas Jefferson, Autobiography (1743–1790)[1]

Thomas Jefferson's brief depiction of two quite different men, George Washington and Benjamin Franklin, captures the characteristics they had in common—humility in public forums, mature wisdom, and sharp focus and brevity in speech. That Jefferson, esteemed for his eloquence, praised these qualities in Franklin and Washington in his Autobiography speaks to his own character.

Franklin never sought or held high elective office in America, nor, except for a minor edit or two of the Declaration, did he write that document or the Constitution. Yet, his patriotic contributions to Philadelphia and the nation were unmatched. Philadelphia was the largest city in America, its cultural and political hub, and for ten years, the nation's first capital. Franklin served as the essential diplomat in Europe responsible for securing the military support and intervention of France, Spain, and other countries, without which, as Washington himself said, the prospects of victory were slim. This is not to say that England might not, on its own, have tired of the hassles of keeping America as its largest and most rebellious colony. Franklin also hatched and found nourishment for the civic institutions that were America's "firsts." He was a master of wit and wisdom.

Franklin was an influential Pennsylvania representative in the Continental Congress during the Revolution and, at eighty-one, the senior delegate at the Constitutional Convention in 1787. In many ways, he was the quintessence of America, which is why Americans have always had a special love for, and affinity with, him.

23

The National Park Service has recently completed an appropriate expansion of the museum at the site of Franklin's home and place of business on Market Street in Philadelphia. The number of ideas, inventions, accomplishments, friendships, and lessons associated with this man is beyond counting. Franklin happily retains his place as America's unparalleled civic-institution builder and prototype of the Renaissance man, learning and mastering a dizzying array of tasks from inventing a wood stove to writing a state constitution to consorting with the monarchs and nobility of Europe and negotiating treaties.

Of special interest to us is that he reached the highs without ever losing an ounce of his identity with the common man. The critical importance of a strong, expanding middle class had been Aristotle's main precept for having a healthy republic. Rousseau and the Founders embraced it in the eighteenth century. In the twentieth century, Theodore Roosevelt, Franklin Roosevelt, and Harry Truman were strong proponents of the principle. Actually, until the Neoconservatives arrived in the 1980's, it was fundamental to all American political thought.

Benjamin Franklin has been called the "personification of the middle class,"[2] and he certainly championed the middle class in his civic ventures in Philadelphia and the Constitutional Convention.

Franklin attended a good grammar school in Boston, but was unable to proceed with formal education, even to the twelfth grade, because of lack of funds. Harvard College remained for him an unfulfilled dream. He went to work in his brother's publishing house in Boston and began a life-long process of self-education. As a young adolescent he departed from Boston for Philadelphia, alone, to forge his future. He learned early in his life the difference between easy promises and genuine commitment. A prominent Pennsylvanian had given him letters of introduction to men of position in London, but when he arrived, the introductions proved to be of little worth. He soon returned to Philadelphia, set up his own printing shop on Market Street, and moved upward and outward from there.

He was constantly improving himself and remembering his roots and the circumstances of the less fortunate in society. We will see later how Franklin, the senior spokesman at the Convention, kept the delegates on course toward establishing a genuine democracy. Actually, he began building America long before the legal foundation was laid in 1787. In 1727 Franklin and his friend William Maugridge, who lived in one of the small houses of a "middling sort" on tiny Elfreth's Alley in Philadelphia, formed a social improvement club, the "Junto," along with ten other men who had shops near the Delaware River docks.[3] The name "Junto" is derived from the Latin verb "to join"[4] and refers to becoming a member of this small society. These philosopher mechanics met weekly after doing some self-assigned homework—readings in philosophy, literature, politics, business, and science.[5] In 1731 Franklin established the first lending library, the Library Company of Philadelphia. Franklin followed up with the formation of the predecessor to the University of Pennsylvania, the Pennsylvania Hospital, a fire insurance company, and the American Philosophical Society—all firsts. The natural sciences and the social sciences were constantly intermingled in his mind and his ventures. Franklin, although lacking formal education, was, himself, the best advertisement for an immersion in the broad liberal arts and for a Renaissance-man life.

At the Convention Franklin spoke to the issue of whether property and wealth should be prerequisites for holding public office, voting, or playing a significant role as an American leader. He had nothing to say in defense of this practice, common in Europe, and instead commented that some of the worst rogues he had known were "the richest rogues."[6] He followed Aristotle's views on the baneful influence of wealth in politics and the importance of virtue. Franklin commented that when avarice and ambition are combined in the same person and that person is promoted to high position, one should expect "the most violent Effect."[7] It was a succinct condemnation of our political system today.

At the end of the Convention Madison recorded in his *Notes* Franklin's comment that he had been looking at the back of the president's chair and constantly wondering whether the image of the sun engraved there was a rising or a setting sun. Franklin said he was now able to conclude, to his own satisfaction, that it—the sun, a symbol of the republic—was rising, not setting. Throughout the Convention, Franklin had a good ear for the concerns of the delegates, and he carefully timed his own replies. His speech at the end of the

Convention was powerful because of its brevity, sincerity, and good sense. He confessed that he had had doubts along the way regarding certain clauses in the Constitution, but he said, in a modest way, that upon reflection, he was not persuaded of his "own rightness as to all matters." He stressed the urgency of the moment, a moment that might not come again, and he called for a unanimous vote in favor of the Constitution.

As to the functioning of the republic, Franklin's views were also very similar to Washington's and Madison's. He said:

> [T]here is no form of government but what may be a blessing to the people if well administered; and I believe, farther, that this [government] is likely to be well administered for a course of years, and can only end in Despotism, as other forms have done before it, when the people shall become so corrupted as to need despotic government, being incapable of any other.[8]

Franklin thus became the first great American to use the words "despotism" and "corruption" together in reference to a potentially negative outcome of the new republic.

A Maryland delegate to the Convention, Dr. James McHenry, kept his own diary of the proceedings and recounted the following anecdote on September 18 that apparently occurred as Franklin was recessing from the State House:

"A lady asked Dr. Franklin Well Doctor what have we got a republic or monarchy [sic]. A republic replied the Doctor if you can keep it. [McHenry followed with this note.] The lady here alluded to was Mrs Powel of Philada. [Mr. Powel served as mayor of the city]."[9]

Franklin's phrase "a republic if you can keep it" has resounded ever since—but not loudly enough.

---

[1] Thomas Jefferson, *The Writings of Thomas Jefferson—Autobiography, 1743–1790* (New York: Putnam, 1914), 90.

[2] Richard Lacayo, *Benjamin Franklin: An Illustrated History of his Life and Times* (New York: TIME Books, 2010).

[3] George W. Boudreau, *Independence: A Guide to Historic Philadelphia* (Yardley, PA: Westholme Publishing, 2012), 233–34.

[4] National Humanities Center, "Benjamin Franklin's Junto Club & Lending Library of Philadelphia founded 1727 & 1731," *Resources Toolbox—*

Becoming American: The British Atlantic Colonies 1690–1763;
http://nationalhumanitiescenter.org.
   [5] Boudreau.
   [6] *Madison's Notes*, III, 1285.
   [7] Benjamin Franklin, *Madison's Notes*, 770–71.
   [8] Benjamin Franklin, *Madison's Notes,* 1652.
   [9] James McHenry, *Papers of Dr. James McHenry on the Federal Convention of 1787*, September 1787, *Avalon,* 18.

Chapter 4

Forming a More Perfect Union

"The great desideratum [goal] in Government is such a modification of the Sovereignty as will render it sufficiently neutral between the different interests and factions, to control one part of the Society from invading the rights of another, and at the same time sufficiently controlled itself, from setting up an interest adverse to that of the whole Society."

—*James Madison, Vices of the Political System of the United States (April, 1787).*[1]

In this chapter we examine the writing of the United States Constitution from May into September, 1787, in Philadelphia. Some of the most important insights that the Founders made were not recorded in the Constitution itself, but in James Madison's *Notes,*[2] a daily record of the proceedings, and in a variety of letters, diaries, and, in the case of Adams and Madison, two rough essays or ruminations written before the Convention. Adams's rumination we addressed in Chapter 1. Remarkably, in Madison's *Vices of the Political System of the United States,*[3] written a month before the Convention, he foresaw dangerous threats that the American republic would encounter centuries later. Then, immediately after the Convention, he elaborated on them in formal essays published as letters in a newspaper—the *Federalist Papers.* Madison used the word "vices" as if America were a living person with vices and virtues; the Founders had a deep personal feeling regarding the new republic to which they were giving birth.

In *Vices* Madison identified two great threats: demagoguery, that we discuss in detail later, and factionalism, the formation of competing and interfering groups or factions that subvert the course of governance.[4] Madison expanded on his analysis of factions in the famous *Federalist Paper* No. 10, and for the purposes of clarity and convenience here, we will refer here to excerpts from both *Vices* and *Federalist Paper* No. 10. Jefferson and Adams (both of whom were absent from the Convention because they were in Europe) endorsed

Madison to become the leader of the delegates in the drafting and negotiating the provisions of the Constitution. Thus, Madison has become known as the "father of the Constitution." George Washington was appointed President of the Convention.

Madison was well prepared for his role by his personal study of historical and philosophical texts, and he was a political centrist not tied to platforms of either of the two emergent political parties, the Federalists and the Democratic-Republicans. As we see again and again in the contemporary writings and speeches of these men, the political rivalry of Alexander Hamilton and Thomas Jefferson and other Founders did not undermine their personal devotion to the same fundamental set of principles. This is an important point of distinction between the nature of politics then and now. In fact, some of the quotations from Hamilton and Jefferson that are presented here are mutually reinforcing. These leaders did not sacrifice the good of the republic to the demagogic behavior that small-minded politicians today use to draw attention to themselves.

Madison's writing style, as we see in the quotation above, was of the eighteenth century, and needs some interpretation for the modern reader. The Latin word "desideratum" means a thing to be desired above others, i.e., a primary goal. When Madison refers to "Government," he means, of course, our federal government. The primary goal of government, then, is a modification of sovereignty (political rule) that will "render it sufficiently neutral between the different interests and factions, to control one part of the Society from invading the rights of another, and at the same time sufficiently controlled itself, from setting up an interest adverse to that of the whole Society." Madison was saying that the primary goal is to prevent factions from invading the rights of other people or setting up themselves as adverse or hostile to the whole society; the key is to modify political rule to achieve neutrality with regard to society as a whole. The majority of the elected representatives of the people must act to promote the *long-term good of the people as a whole and the republic itself.* Throughout their writings the Founders repeat that the primary goal of government must be to achieve the "happiness" of the citizens, not groups or factions. As we will see, America has strayed a very long way from its fundamental purpose

Madison defined faction as "a number of citizens... united and actuated by the same common impulses of passion, or of interest, adverse to the rights of other citizens, or to the permanent and aggregate interests of the community."[5] George Washington despised factions as much as Madison, and he demonstrated his strong beliefs during his presidency by refusing to join *either* political party and by refusing to take the fledgling republic to war as the factions demanded. John Adams, Washington's Vice President, was passionately— sometimes explosively—devoted to the same principle and to Washington's legacy.

Madison in *Federalist Paper* No. 10 took the analysis a few steps further. He said that it is in the nature of man that parties "become inflamed with mutual animosity."[6] (Here he echoed Aristotle.) The most common and "durable" source of factions is the "various and unequal distribution of property," he said.[7] (Wealth distribution is the subject of a later chapter.) In the face of Madison's statements, it is impossible to argue that taking steps now to restore the proper wealth distribution is "un-American."[8]

In studying factionalism, Madison concluded that while it would be impossible to eliminate the *causes* of factionalism in a democracy, it was definitely possible to control the evils it produces by controlling its *effects:*

"The regulation of these various and interfering interests forms the principal task of modern legislation and involves the spirit of party and faction in the necessary and ordinary operations of government."[9]

It is a sign of Madison's priorities that he considered the regulation of special interests and gross wealth imbalance to be the *principal* task of modern legislation. Reducing or eliminating the internal threat to the republic from factionalism was top priority.

It is sometimes said that America has outgrown the Founders' republic, that there are just too many people with too many different interests, ethnic and racial backgrounds, and so forth. The alternative is never clear—and surely not good. Madison believed just the opposite. Rather than considering pluralism an obstacle or fatal threat, Madison considered it an advantage because theoretically at least there would be less chance for any single faction or combination of factions to dominate and a greater chance of being able to sift the general population for leaders and to train worthy representatives for public office. Madison's view has failed because the political system has been corrupted more thoroughly than even he anticipated and because America ignored the Founders' urgent call for high-quality, universal education of the common people in the arts and humanities, civics, and ethics.

Madison envisioned the development of a process of elections that will extract from the mass of society "the purest and noblest characters which it contains."[10] The process would include the training of, and reaching out to, potential representatives of the people. It was not enough to sit back and wait to see what candidates came to the fore—and certainly not to hinge their success on their enrichment with millions of dollars.

One issue at the Convention was mishandled, and the mishandling led to the failure of Madison's plan. An impressive number of major Founders favored imposing limits on the successive re-election of all candidates, i.e., term limits.[11] Elbridge Gerry, John Rutledge, and Pierce Butler flatly opposed allowing re-election to the same office.[12] John Adams, we have seen, believed that legislators, left to their own devices, would become abusive of authority, obsessed with personal gain and glory ("ravenous beasts"), and need to be returned to private life to gain empathy with the people and basic humility. He was absent from the Convention, but it is most unlikely that Madison and the delegates from Massachusetts were ignorant of Adams' views. Even more compelling was that Jefferson (also in Europe) and George Mason, the two leading scholar-Founders from Madison's home state, strongly opposed unlimited re-election.

In December 1787, during the debates on state ratification of the Constitution, Thomas Jefferson wrote a letter directly to Madison from Paris saying:

"The second feature I dislike, and *greatly dislike*, is the abandonment in every instance of the necessity of rotation in office, and most particularly in the case of the President."[13]

Jefferson's "great" personal dislike for having no term limits, conveyed in a personal letter to Madison during the ratification period, should have tipped the scales on this issue for Madison and caused Madison to amend the proposed Constitution before final ratification.

Madison did not react. Ironically, the last word was spoken, or rather written, by the State of Rhode Island, which had sent no delegates to the Convention. It did submit a ratification document in May 1790 demanding that legislators be restrained from oppression by being "reduced to a private station, returned into the mass of the people" at fixed periods.[14]

Madison *himself* distrusted legislators and had said that past experience demonstrates "a powerful tendency of the Legislature to absorb all power into its vortex."[15] He emphasized that goodness in politics comes from a *"multiplicity* of views, absent corruption,"[16] and he wrote in *Federalist Paper* No. 37 that "[t]he genius of republican liberty seems to demand on one side not only that all power should be derived from the people, but that those intrusted with it should be kept in dependence on the people by a short duration of their appointments."[17] All signs, therefore, pointed to the insertion of a provision establishing term limits, but it failed to happen.

When we approach the Constitution and attempt to extract a set of authentic, original principles against which to measure America's performance, we must understand who the Founders really were. It is true that all of the fifty-five delegates were male and of European descent, but this, of course, was a reflection of the demographics and the prevailing culture at the time. We must take a closer look. There was plenty of heated debate at the Convention, and this flowed not just from personalities, but from a diversity of backgrounds and interests. Some delegates were from the North and others from the South, some had mercantile backgrounds and others had agricultural ones, some were from small states and others from large ones, and some were very young and others much older. The youngest two delegates were George Mason (26) and Charles Pinckney (29). For many reasons, not all fifty-five attended the four-month marathon. Thirty-nine delegates signed the Constitution in September before handing it over to the states for ratification.

There is no way of quantifying the significance of the Philadelphia *City Tavern* in the building of our nation, but it is sure that delegates at the end of their long, hot daily sessions did go off to the Tavern for drinks and dinner, and they continued discussions. Independence

National Park did the right thing by ensuring that the Tavern was authentically rebuilt and opened to patrons.

The background of Alexander Hamilton, to the extent that we know it from scraps here and there, was extraordinary. He was born in the West Indies out of wedlock to a Scotsman, originally of some means but soon bankrupt, and a French mother. His mother died when Hamilton was thirteen; his father had already abandoned the family. Hamilton was an orphan. He learned some Hebrew at a Jewish school. He taught himself the Greek and Roman classics, as well as French. He emigrated to America at sixteen and obtained a Bachelor of Arts degree at nineteen from King's College, later Columbia University. He was brilliant and began writing political essays in his teenage years. He fought for General Washington in the Revolution, and later he became his trusted advisor and Secretary of the Treasury.[18]

Hamilton went through political changes, reportedly commencing with his military service. In his youth he was a passionate, even radical, advocate for democracy; in his own words, he was "inviolably attached to the essential rights of mankind and the true interests of society"—the rights to freedom and the pursuit of happiness.[19] Later, he stressed that the federal government should be strong and vigorous. He led the Federalist Party into rivalry with Jefferson's party. Jefferson is America's greatest democrat. He went through similar changes. Jefferson once favored an appointed senate instead of an elected one, but later he grew more and more committed to educating and empowering the people.[20] One of the inspiring characteristics of the Founders is that, despite shifts in opinions and differences among them on some issues, it is clear from their writings and speeches that they were united on the big issues.

George Washington was President of the Convention. He confessed "an ardent love for my Country" in his First Inaugural.[21] When Washington became president, he set a model for future holders of public office by repeatedly seeking "information from all quarters," making decisions "more independently than any man I ever saw,"[22] and firmly rejecting calls for him to remain for a third term.

The setting for the Convention was the cluster of colonial and Georgian buildings from approximately Eighth Street in Philadelphia east to the Delaware River (Front Street takes the place of First Street), and more precisely, the Pennsylvania State House (now, Independence Hall) and its appendages east of Sixth Street—and, of course, the City Tavern.

Madison noted on the first day that "Doctor Franklin alone would have been thought a competitor [to Washington for president]", but he was infirm and on that day confined to his home and he (Franklin) personally supported the selection of Washington. The note reflects the tremendous respect that the delegates had for Franklin.

Twelve states sent delegates. Rhode Island misjudged the willingness of its sister states to find a good balance that would protect the rights of smaller states; therefore, it boycotted the Convention. It was a mistake that the next-smallest state, Delaware, did not make. Rhode Island finally ratified the Constitution in 1790 on the understanding that the Bill of Rights essentially as submitted by George Mason would become the first ten amendments. The smallest state was being faithful to its tradition as the protector of individual rights and freedoms (especially of religion).

One of the surprises in the record of the proceedings is the contribution made by Charles Pinckney of South Carolina. He switched from the Federalist Party to become a Jeffersonian Democratic-Republican. At the beginning of the Convention, Pinckney offered a barebones draft of the Constitution that included elements of the final version usually attributed to more well-known founders. More importantly, Pinckney had his own vision of the political and social structure of America. He was a strong proponent of the middle class and believed as deeply as Franklin that the health of the republic depended on doing whatever was needed to maintain the health of the middle class and to promote a sense of mutual respect among Americans of different social classes. Pinckney said:

[T]he people of the United States are more equal in their circumstances than the people of any other country... they have very few rich men among them—by rich I mean those whose riches may have a dangerous influence, or such as are esteemed in Europe... [I]t is not probable that their number will be greatly increased.[23]

Pinckney's description of America at the time was undoubtedly accurate. America was not dominated by European-style aristocrats or wealthy nobility. Even fifty years later, a French aristocrat fascinated with the American democracy, Alexis de Tocqueville, wrote that: "Almost all Americans are comfortable... there are few rich."[24] In Pinckney's view, this was one of America's greatest assets. Unfortunately, Pinckney erred in his prognostication for the future. The "dangerous influence" of riches that Pinckney feared became reality.

Pinckney identified three classes in America: professionals, merchants, and people with interests in land. He viewed each of them as mutually interdependent. This appreciation of the mutual interdependence of the classes is essential for a proper balance in government and society. In Pinckney's eyes, America was "one great and equal body of citizens."[25] From a civics standpoint, this vision squared well with Aristotle's concept of a healthy representative democracy and also with the vision that the Founders finally adopted at the end of the summer of 1787.

Overall, Madison performed brilliantly. He supported the Virginia Plan, but was open to modifications. He proposed that the legislature contain two independent houses of different sizes selected by different methods; the upper body would give every state two senators, and the lower body would allot representatives according to population. The senate had the "advise and consent power" that enabled it to block a presidential appointment to the executive branch or the judiciary if the candidate was unfit and did not possess the requisite virtues. Federal judges were to be insulated from the political fray by lifetime appointments to the bench. The people had the power to elect the representatives and the president and vice president. (The so-called Electoral College was intended to serve as a helpful intermediary in the election of the chief executive). The powers of the three branches were divided and specified in the first three Articles of the Constitution.

It was important to Madison—and all the Founders—to plant John Locke's principle of popular sovereignty firmly in the foundation of this new government while at the same time establishing a mechanism for elected and appointed representatives to govern day to day, to apply their wisdom and virtue, and to be held responsible for failure. One aspect of popular sovereignty was the Founders' creation of an *alternate* means of calling a Convention to amend the Constitution: a Convention can be called either by a super-majority vote of Congress *or* by a vote of two-thirds of the state legislatures.[26] As Locke said and as the Founders reiterated in many writings and speeches, it was vital for the people to retain ultimate power to alter or abolish any part of government that became corrupted and no longer served the public good.

While America's Constitution remains the greatest written constitution for any democratic republic in history, the Founders had no illusions that their work product was perfect or immutable. They made it clear that they relied upon future generations to become educated in civics and the humanities, to exercise reason, to become informed of current events, to cull from the general population and groom for public office certain persons of virtue, and ultimately to follow Locke and Jefferson by reforming or eliminating any part of the body politic that no longer served the public good.

Thus, by the end of 1787, America had in place a set of principles and a structure for a great, well-balanced democratic republic.

---

[1] James Madison, *Vices of the Political System of the United States,* (April, 1787), reproduced in *Founders Online* by the National Archives; http://founders.archives.gov/documents/Madison (hereafter "*Vices, Founders Online*"). See also, "Vices of the Political System," *James Madison—Writings* (New York: The Library of America—The Literary Classics of the United States, 1999), 79, and *James Madison to George Washington April 1787: Vices of the Political System of the United States* (National Humanities Center, 2010), 7; www.nationalhumanitiescenter.org.

[2] James Madison, *The Papers of James Madison, and his Reports of Debates in the Federal Convention,* ed. Henry D. Gilpin (Washington, DC: Langtree & O'Sullivan, 1840). Also, *Notes on the Debates in the Federal Convention of 1787 Reported by James Madison;* http://avalon.law.yale.edu/subject_menus/18th .asp.

[3] *Vices, Founders Online.*

[4] Id., 11.1 and 11.2.

[5] *Federalist*, Mentor, 78–79.

[6] Id.

[7] Id.

[8] Citation in chapter below.

[9] Id.

[10] *Vices, Founders Online,* 369.

---

[11] *Notes*, II, 1498. 1595.

[12] Id.

[13] Jefferson, "To James Madison From Thomas Jefferson, 20 December 1787, Paris," *Founders Online,* National Archives, 26 (italics mine); http://founders.archives.gov/documents/Madison.

[14] http://www.usconstitution.net/rat_ri.html.

[15] *Notes,* II, 1163.

[16] Vices, *Founders Online,* 369.

[17] *Federalist*, Mentor, No. 37, 227.

[18] William Graham Sumner and Robert Henry Thurston, *Alexander Hamilton,* Google Play (formerly Google Books); https://play.google.com/books.

[19] Darren Staloff, *Hamilton, Adams and Jefferson—The Politics of the Enlightenment and the American Founding* (New York: Hill & Wang, 2005), 57–61.

[20] Ibid. See also Bruce Chadwick, *The Story of the Unlikely Alliance that Saved the Constitution and the Nation* New York: Sourcebooks, 2009).

[21] George Washington, "First Inaugural Address—April 30, 1789," collected in The Library of America, *American Speeches: The Revolution to the Civil War* (New York: Literary Classics of the United States, 2006.

[22] David McCullough, John Adams (New York: Simon & Schuster, 2001), 415.

[23] *Notes*, II, 949.

[24] Alexis de Tocqueville, *Democracy in America* (Chicago: University of Chicago Press, 2000), 51.

[25] *Notes*, II, 949.

[26] Constitution, Art. V.

Chapter 5

Theodore Roosevelt–The Progressive Conservative

"The future of our country will depend upon having men... of sincerity and truth, of unshakeable conviction, of power, of personality, with the spirit of Justice and the fighting spirit through all the generations; and the mightiest service that can be seen today to accomplish that for our country is to make it impossible that Theodore Roosevelt, his teaching and his personality shall be forgotten. Oh, that we might have him with us now!"
—*Elihu Root (1919)*[1]

In September 1901 Vice President Theodore Roosevelt suddenly became President upon the assassination of William McKinley. No man since the Founders has embodied as fully and communicated as fervently the essence of America as Theodore Roosevelt. Interestingly, as America has declined in recent years, there has been an outpouring of well-written Roosevelt biographies.[2] Americans have been fascinated and energized by these stories, but they have not grasped Roosevelt's greatest contribution—his lessons in civics—nor acted upon them. This failure must be rectified.

Elihu Root, whose words appear above, was the quintessential great American statesman of Roosevelt's era. His name is not as familiar to us as it should be. He held many high public offices—from the prestigious position of United States Attorney for the Southern District of New York (Manhattan) to Secretary of War, Secretary of State, and United States Senator. He was a brilliant lawyer, co-founder of the American Law Institute, founder of the Council on Foreign Relations, recipient of the Nobel Peace Prize in 1912, and a close friend and admirer of Roosevelt. In his opinion Roosevelt was the "greatest teacher of the essentials of popular self-government the world had ever known... the deep fundamental truths of public life, of a great self-governing democracy, the eternal truths upon which justice and liberty must depend among men."[3] The "future of our country," Root said, depends on listening to, and following, Roosevelt.

Roosevelt was challenged early in life by health problems; he responded by becoming a physical and mental trainer for himself. He suffered debilitating episodes of depression. He discovered that retreats to nature provided the most reliable form of therapy. Roosevelt was a self-taught naturalist of major distinction, especially with regard to birds, and a rugged hiker, camper, and survivalist.[4] He became a close friend of the nation's first great conservationist, John Muir, and the two went on retreat in the west. Roosevelt's boundless curiosity and appreciation of the natural environment is comparable to that of Thomas Jefferson and his famous Lewis and Clark Expedition. Moreover, Roosevelt's stamina and physical courage are legendary; he was often on the cusp of physical recklessness.

It was fortunate for America that such a man brought these qualities to his political life and married them to an unwavering devotion to the ethics and the fundamental principles of the Founders.

Roosevelt served in office for seven and a half years. The Republican Party at that time was supportive of Roosevelt because he was a rugged individualist, well established in the social class of the most successful Republican entrepreneurs, and a powerful advocate for the American ideals of freedom and justice. Partway through his presidency, however, Roosevelt began to notice the emergence of a new group of Republicans calling themselves "Conservatives," who found Roosevelt's ceaseless campaigning for social reforms and federal protection of wild natural places threatening to their own status as capitalists. The Conservatives claimed that *they* were the ones representing the American ideals of freedom and the pursuit of happiness. Roosevelt perceived quite the opposite to be true.

The Conservatives represented a small percentage of Americans who pursued and, in many cases achieved, enormous wealth, status and power through the vehicle of giant trusts (corporations) at a time when there were few—or no—effective government restraints on business. Roosevelt quipped that the only thing these men wanted to conserve was their own wealth and status. Roosevelt appears to be the first—and only—American president to apply the Aristotelian word "plutocracy" to America.[5] A century later, in 2015, this observation is more compelling than it was then, notwithstanding the existence of many laws, regulations, and policies aimed at protecting the people from precisely that fate.

In his *Autobiography* Roosevelt spoke freely regarding the so-called Conservatives:

> If we examine the battle cry of political polemics, we find that it is based upon the conception of the divine right of property, and the pre-occupation [prior occupation] by older or more favored or more alert or richer men or nations, of territory, of the forces of nature, of machinery, of all the functions of what we call civilization.[6]

Roosevelt's swipe at the peddlers of a "divine right of property" (based on prior occupation of that property) would have incurred passionate support from the Founders. The fact that the trademarks of an ugly plutocracy existed in 1900 and proliferated in 2016 would have enraged and deeply disappointed the Founders. The same aim inspired the "Occupy Wall Street" movement a few years ago, but that movement lacked the educational base, leadership, organization, and sophistication of the grass-roots movements of the 1970's—and it soon wilted. Roosevelt drew an analogy between the barons of industry and the *feudal barons* from medieval times in Europe and their fiefdoms:

> The big reactionaries of the business world and their allies and instruments among politicians and newspaper editors took advantage of this division of opinion [between complete freedom for industry and eradication of corporations, neither of which Roosevelt favored], and... demanded for themselves an immunity from governmental control, which if granted would have been as wicked and as foolish as immunity to the barons of the twelfth century... There have been aristocracies which have played a great and beneficent part in the stages of growth of mankind; but we had come to the stage where for our people what was needed was a real democracy; and of all

the forms of tyranny the least attractive and the most vulgar is
the tyranny of mere wealth, the *tyranny of plutocracy*.[7]

This quotation shows a depth of insight into the workings of the
republic shortly after the turn of the twentieth century that no one else
then—or later—has displayed or had the courage to display. Roosevelt
sketched a "corrupt alliance" that has come to full flower only in the
last thirty years. The business reactionaries who sought everything for
themselves as if they were feudal barons did not operate alone. They
worked in conjunction with politicians and members of the news media
who had something to gain by attaching themselves to the capitalists
and their demagoguery.

Roosevelt became the first—and only—American president, to my
knowledge, to sound the alarm against an outbreak of *plutocracy*, the
"least attractive" and "most vulgar" form of tyranny. Roosevelt
perceived where this destructive movement was heading. It was the
worst form of corruption that America could suffer because it thrived
on demagoguery, the misleading of the people, and the people held the
ultimate political authority.

Roosevelt acknowledged that during America's western expansion,
rugged individualism and self-reliance were an esteemed and necessary
part of America's growth. But those early days had passed. Roosevelt's
own political success had been in no small part attributable to wide
respect for his personal courage and dynamism, strength of conviction,
and unshakeable devotion to principles, i.e., rugged individualism. And
yet now he recognized that in business and politics there had developed
a "riot of individualistic materialism under which complete freedom for
the individual... turned out in practice to mean perfect freedom for the
strong to wrong the weak."[8] No one has said it better. The delicate
balance in politics, government, and society on which the Founders
depended was being upset.

Roosevelt wrote the following:

Corrupt business and corrupt politics act and react, with ever
increasing debasement, one on the other... The "business"
which is hurt by the movement for honesty is the kind of
business, which in the long run, it pays the country to have

hurt. It is the kind of business which has tended to make the very name "high finance" a term of scandal to which all honest men of business should join in putting an end.[9]

Again, the barons of business and finance were not acting alone, as we will see in the Savings & Loan scandal of the early 1980's that marked the beginning of the "avalanche of malfeasance." Roosevelt, perhaps more than anyone, dissected the vicious cycle. Corrupt business and corrupt politics acted and reacted. Industry, of course, attacked Roosevelt and threatened that if he pursued his reforms, the people would suffer in the end. It was the same demagoguery that followers of former President Ronald Reagan disseminated when they argued that the rich had to be made richer in order to "trickle down" some of the wealth to the people. Theodore Roosevelt already knew, almost a century in advance, that when the plutocrats *are* given what they really want, they will simply grab for more; the people will suffer, not benefit. He was bold in campaigning for honesty, fair-dealing, and justice—and not succumbing to the threats. Roosevelt said:

> But if it were true that to cut out rottenness from the body politic meant a momentary check to an unhealthy seeming prosperity, I should not for one moment hesitate to put the knife to the cancer… [I]t is necessary to insist upon honesty in business and politics alike, in all walks of life, in big things and in little things.[10]

Part of Roosevelt's appeal is that he was bold in supporting what was right long before his causes won popular approval. He called for federal regulation of stock offerings, full disclosure of corporate financial conditions, minimum wages, Social Security, supporting the middle and working classes, women's suffrage, *a ban on corporate contributions to political campaigns,* the detailed reporting of monies lawfully received for campaigning, and a measure of public financing to eliminate the political debts that Aristotle had predicted would destroy a republic.[11]

Finally, Roosevelt was our greatest environmental-conservation president. He created the first *fifty-one* national wildlife refuges and was able to secure a new statute from Congress that enabled him to designate eighteen national monuments by executive order, a statute used to great advantage by many conservation-minded successors (and perennially attacked by Republicans). In March 1909 Senator Robert M. LaFollette of Wisconsin wrote an article that captured Roosevelt's spirit and accomplishment in this area:

> This globe is the capital stock of the race. It is just so much coal and oil and gas. This may be economized or wasted. The same thing is true of phosphates and other mineral resources... Our forests have been destroyed; they must be restored. Our soils have been depleted; they must be built up and conserved. These questions are not of this day only or of this generation. They belong all to the future. Their conservation requires that high moral tone which regards the earth as a posterity to whom we owe a sacred duty. This immense idea Roosevelt, with high statesmanship, dinned into the ears of the Nation until the Nation heeded... Nothing can be greater or finer than this.[12]

It was not until the 1970's that this "immense idea" really found its way into the hearts and minds of the American people and their political representatives. Roosevelt took his place alongside Madison as one of America's wisest seers when the Environmental Renaissance sprung forth in the 1970's—and later, when giant corporations collapsed under an avalanche of malfeasance and dragged the financial security of the nation and its people down with them.

---

[1]Elihu Root, "Theodore Roosevelt," *The North American Review,* November, 1919, 754, reproduced in Old Magazine Articles; http://www.oldmagazinearticles.com.

[2] Geoffrey C. Ward & Ken Burns, *The Roosevelts: An Intimate History* (New York: Knopf, 2014); Ken Burns film of the same name: PBS, 2014. Doris Kearns Goodwin, *The Bully Pulpit—Theodore Roosevelt, William Howard Taft, and the Golden Age of Journalism* (New York: Simon & Schuster, 2013). Edmund Morris, *Theodore Rex* (New York: Modern Library, 2002). Edmund Morris, *The Rise of Theodore Roosevelt* (New York: Modern Library, 2001). Gerard Helferich, *Theodore Roosevelt and the Assassin* (Guilford, CT: 2013). Edward J. Renehan, Jr., *The Lion's Pride* (New York: Oxford University Press,

1998). David McCullough, *Mornings on Horseback* (New York: Simon & Schuster, 1981).

[3] Root.

[4] See, Candice Millard, *The River of Doubt: Theodore Roosevelt's Darkest Journey* (New York: Anchor Books, 2006).

[5] Roosevelt used the term conspicuously in his Eighth Annual Message to Congress on December 8, 1908. Eighth Annual Message to Congress, TeachingAmericanHistory.org; http:/teachingamericanhistory.org /library/document.

[6] *Theodore Roosevelt: An Autobiography* (New York: MacMillan, 1913), XV, App. A, 15, reproduced in Bartleby.com (1999), http://bartleby.com/55/. Page citations are from Bartleby.

[7] Id. at XII, 4 (italics mine).

[8] Id. at XII, 1.

[9] Id. at XII, 54-55, Roosevelt letter to Attorney General Charles Bonaparte, 2 January 1908.

[10] Id. at XII, 59.

[11] Sixth and Seventh Annual Messages to Congress, December 3, 1906 and December 3, 1907, respectively. TeachingAmericanHistory.org.

[12] Robert M. LaFollette, "Article on Theodore Roosevelt's Accomplishments (March 1909)," collected in Roosevelt's *Autobiography*, X, 60, n. 1.

Chapter 6

America Resilient in Crisis—The 1970's

"If we have wisdom to make the best use of the advantages with which we are now favored, we cannot fail, under the just administration of a good government, to become a great and a happy people."

—*Letter of George Washington to the Touro Synagogue Congregation, Newport, Rhode Island (1790)*[1]

President Washington's letter to the Touro Synagogue Congregation in 1790 exhibited his strong personal commitment to religious liberty a year before the freedoms in the Bill of Rights were added to the Constitution. The circumstances of this letter are interesting. Rhode Island had shunned the Constitutional Convention—following the state's tradition of dissenting. Washington was now America's first president, and he was a passionate believer in the union of states. He waited until Rhode Island ratified the Constitution—admittedly with a list of conditions that included the adoption of the Bill of Rights—before reaching out to the laggard state. However, rather than expressing any criticism of the state's behavior, Washington, an Anglican Church member and Virginia plantation owner, scheduled a personal visit with Secretary of State Thomas Jefferson and others to the Touro Synagogue. Touro is now the oldest Jewish synagogue in America and a handsome building in Newport designed by a prominent architect.

Washington was warmly received by the Touro warden, Moses Seixas, and thanked for his courageous leadership. The event was an instant success. Inclusivity was effortless and genuine on the part of Washington and his colleagues. Washington's goal for America was *"a great and happy people,"* and he meant it.

At the same time, it is noteworthy that Washington prefaced his vision of a great and happy people with the conditional "if": "If we have wisdom to make the best use of the advantages with which we are now favored, we cannot fail, under the just administration of a good government, to become a great and a happy people." The republic did have wonderful advantages, but they would fade away if the people did not employ *wisdom* to make the best use of them and *take action* to ensure the just administration of a good government. The attainment of the goals that Jefferson and Washington enunciated—and that have become iconic in America—would be frustrated by failure or refusal to follow the specific steps laid out for education, civic engagement, and, as Jefferson said, the alert, thorough censoring of our governors.

Americans have not educated their people, naturalized a flood of immigrants, deported those unfit or unwilling to become U.S. citizens, censored their governors, employed wisdom to make the best use of our advantages, or brought about the just administration of a good government. A good way of teaching the importance of Washington's lesson is to locate in the patient history of America an episode when major crises severely tested the republic's resilience and the republic *overcame* the crises. The period from 1969 to 1979 fits this description. There are advantages in selecting this period for a lesson in civics.

First, it is not ancient history, and therefore, it is more easily compared to the present. There have been great demographic changes since then, mostly because of unprecedented immigration (the subject of a later chapter), but those changes do not render the Founders' design archaic or obsolete. The great failures since the 1970's have arisen from money corruption of the political system and abandonment of the fundamental principles, not inadequacy of the original plan.

Second, the crises in the 1970's were huge. They threatened the republic's survival: the often violent struggle for civil rights for African-Americans; the unconstitutional, despotic Vietnam War; and the unconstitutional, despotic Watergate conspiracy and scandal involving almost *two dozen* executive-branch officials, including the president of the United States, his attorney general, and his top White House aides.

Third, America burst forth with the remarkable Environmental Renaissance. This phenomenon I know well because I was an attorney at the U.S. Department of Justice in Washington representing the newly formed Environmental Protection Agency (EPA) and working closely with members of all three branches of government.

Finally, I am not alone in holding the view that this period was the last time when America truly functioned as the republic that the Founders designed. In 2012 New York Times writer Frank Rich examined the state of the union and reported that, in his opinion, America had been "comatose" for thirty years.[2] In other words, America had not been healthy and fully functioning since before the 1980's, the date I assign as the onset of the systemic disease.

We will consider the events chronologically. In terms of the crises, the first was the civil rights struggle. It encompassed a wide-ranging, passionate series of events in the South, in Washington, D.C., and around the country. It was the last major step in the long haul from America's Civil War, Lincoln's emancipation, and the passage of the Thirteenth Amendment. When I say "last step," I am referring to major legal and structural steps; vile racism is far from banished within America, and in some respects, it seems to have erupted just at a time when the historic election of Barack Obama to the presidency should have strengthened the nation against racism. The tide turned in favor of civil rights at the end of the 1960's and beginning of the 1970's because the cause was just and quintessentially American, and because there was a people's movement with leaders of courage, determination, eloquence, and the logistical skill to draw masses of citizens to the right place at the right time. The federal civil-rights statutes enacted were clean and crisp; they stand out from hundreds of bloated federal statutes that have been rolling down from Capitol Hill laden with pork projects, special-interest giveaways, and intentional or sloppy ambiguities in the language.

The second crisis was the ten-year war in Vietnam that spread out into Laos and Cambodia under a demagogic American president, Lyndon B. Johnson. We will examine this event more closely in the chapter on disease in the executive branch. Like most demagogic, despotic wars, this one was a horror and a disaster from beginning to end. The only thing right that happened was the unprecedented, successful campaign by the people to force Congress to *repeal* the phony declaration of war known as the Tonkin Bay Resolution.

The third crisis was the Watergate scandal. President Nixon and his top aides, including the Attorney General of the United States, John Mitchell, took a Republican political-campaign "dirty trick" and ballooned it into a high-level, long-running cover-up conspiracy that paralyzed government and the country. There were *dozens* of felony convictions of executive branch officials (including the highest law-enforcement official in the United States), and Nixon was forced to resign. The fabric of the country was torn. At one point I found myself walking to work amidst a May Day demonstration when helicopters landed troops on the Washington Mall and protesters ran next to me, down Constitution Avenue, past the Washington Monument, and toward the Justice Department. Bizarre and shocking ironies sprouted up everywhere.

A corps of journalists, e.g., Bob Woodward, Carl Bernstein and their editor, Ben Bradlee at the Post, Walter Cronkite and Eric Sevareid at CBS News, served as principal mentors to the people, distinguishing right from wrong, delivering the truth, and staying close to America's fundamental principles. The system of checks and balances sprung to life in the human forms of Democratic Senator Sam Ervin and his Special Watergate Committee, including Republican Senator Howard Baker, who was Ervin's Vice Chairman; U.S. District Judge John Sirica, who ruled against Nixon's claim to withhold the Oval Office tape recordings; the Watergate Special Prosecutors; and various Justice Department attorneys, who prosecuted the conspirators. In the end, America reclaimed its status as a government of laws, not men.

Considering the magnitude of overcoming the above-mentioned breakdowns, it seemed unlikely that America, in the same decade, would be capable of embarking on a new epic journey, the Environmental Renaissance. A cross section of Americans participated in this movement: individual conservationists and their groups (many fewer of the latter than exist today), scientists, government officials at all levels, congressmen, federal judges, attorneys and staff at EPA and the Interior Department and other federal departments, attorneys at the Justice Department representing the agencies in court, many ordinary citizens, Supreme Court Justice William O. Douglas, and even on one memorable occasion, the United Nations at its New York headquarters. The story of the U.N. Earth Day celebration on March 21, 1971 gives us a good perspective on this phenomenon.

There is still competition among municipalities as to which Earth Day celebration was the first or most important; spring-equinox celebrations sprang up around the country, and many continue today. It suffices to say pollution of air, water, and land, and destruction of wildlife had reached the point of ripeness for a powerful grass-roots movement in America, not unlike the state of civic decay today.

As the war in Southeast Asia continued on, the Secretary-General of the United Nations decided to ring the Peace Bell in a joint ceremony on March 21 appealing for a halt to the fighting and a re-establishment of harmony between mankind and the planet. There was logic to this juxtaposition—a logic that eludes congressmen on Capitol Hill today. The Secretary-General delivered a proclamation in the form of a pledge that was to be signed by important representatives of America and other countries. The proclamation read, in part, as follows:

> That each signer will (his own conscience being his judge) measure his commitment by how much time and money he gives to these purposes, and realizing the great urgency of the task, he will give freely of his time and money to activities and programmes he believes will best further these Earth renewal purposes. (At least 9 percent of the world's present income is going to activities that support war and spread pollution. Ten percent can tip the balance for healthy peaceful progress.)[3]

The proclamation was an appeal for unity and action among citizens of all nations—and a common understanding of man's fundamental responsibility to cherish and protect the earth and its wild inhabitants. The proclamation is quite similar to Pope Francis's 2015 papal encyclical on climate change and the environment. Pope Francis described a spiral of self-destruction which engulfs us, the critical need for dialogue and transparency, the lack of political will, and the fatal mindset of short-term gain.[4]

The proclamation signers included Senator Hugh Scott of Pennsylvania (the Republican Senate Minority Leader); Senator Mark Hatfield of Oregon (considered as a possible Vice President for Republican Richard Nixon); Democratic Senator Mike Gravel of Alaska (who worked to end the military draft during the Vietnam War); U.S. astronaut Buzz Aldrin and a Russian cosmonaut; scientists from Japan and other countries; John Gardner of Common Cause and David Brower of Friends of the Earth; political representatives of

Mexico, Costa Rica, India, Canada, Palestine (Arafat), France, Egypt, the State of New York, the City of New York (Mayor Dinkins); and the beloved, great violinist Yehudi Menuhin, a Jewish refugee and statesman in his own right. This amalgamation of signers highlights the difference between then and now. Membership in a political faction, the Republican Party for example, did not bind a member to cultist anti-environment ideology aimed at securing political-campaign contributions from industry.

The Environmental Renaissance commenced more or less simultaneously on Capitol Hill with the passage in 1969 of the National Environmental Policy Act (NEPA) and throughout the country in "Earth Day" events. Politicians were intent on *listening* to this impressive diversity of voices. NEPA was an appropriate first step. It required federal agencies having responsibilities for making decisions significantly affecting the quality of the environment to prepare Environmental Impact Statements before making final decisions. The environment was now on the agenda for all federal government decision-making. The lead agencies had to assess reasonable alternatives to a potentially destructive action—including no action at all. The frequently dissenting Supreme Court Justice William O. Douglas had once questioned whether *trees* have legal standing to sue for their own protection. If trees could not speak in court for themselves, who could—and would? NEPA provided a partial answer to this question.

In the early part of the 1970's the former Senate Committee on Public Works handled environmental matters. Democratic Senator Edmund Muskie of Maine sponsored the Clean Air and Water Acts, and Republican Senator Howard Baker of Tennessee was deeply involved in bringing the members of his party into an understanding of the issues and leading them toward final legislative approval. There was a genuine process of education and fact-finding. Congressmen listened to scientists and engineers and forged a legal framework for the long-term good of America and its people.

Howard Baker earned the title of the "Great Conciliator." The Environmental Renaissance could never have happened without the support of the most respected Republicans on the key committee: Baker and later, John Chafee of Rhode Island, who became minority leader of the Senate Committee on the Environment and Public Works. Baker served in the Senate from 1967 to 1985 and only recently died in 2014. Baker also distinguished himself when, as Vice-Chairman of the Watergate Committee, he placed his loyalty to America above his friendship with Richard Nixon and ferreted out the misdeeds of the administration. Nixon actually offered to Baker a seat on the Supreme Court in 1971, but he switched his nomination to William Rehnquist when Baker procrastinated.

Baker performed well. There was not a single nay vote in the Senate on the 1970 Clean Air Act *or* the 1972 Clean Water Act before Nixon vetoed the Water Act on fiscal spending grounds (and was decisively overridden). One of the amazing statistics is that even after Nixon's veto, the House of Representatives voted to override the veto by an overwhelming 247 to 23. It is significant that at his signing of the Clean Air Act in 1970, to which Nixon had no strong fiscal objection, he hailed Theodore Roosevelt and his many environmental accomplishments. Nixon was a conservative republican. He evidently concurred in Roosevelt's definition of true conservatism.

An impressive stream of federal environmental statutes, bold and innovative, poured forth during the following eight years. Even as late as in 1990, Howard Baker supported a monumental amendment to the Clean Air Act that we will discuss later. Briefly, it required the phase-out of chlorofluorocarbons to restore the ozone layer in the stratosphere, the reduction of sulfur dioxide from electric power plants to prevent acid rain, the listing of 189 toxic pollutants to be regulated, certain clean fuel programs, and energy conservation strategies.

Baker successfully opposed a Republican-sponsored Clean Water Act amendment to limit the jurisdiction of the Corps of Engineers in controlling the dredging and filling of wetlands, a proposal that has become a Republican Party obsession despite undisputed findings that restoring wetlands is a top priority to protect New Orleans and other coastal communities from flood disasters.

When Baker supported Jimmy Carter's proposed Panama Canal Treaty, he lost the support of Neoconservatives, specifically Ronald Reagan, who had been leaning toward choosing him instead of Bob Dole as his vice president. Baker said that the Clean Water Act was "far and away the most significant and promising piece of environmental legislation ever enacted by Congress."[5] In 2003, the Howard Baker Center for Public Policy was established at the University of Tennessee.[6] Primary goals of the Center are restoring civil discourse on critical issues and overcoming the demagoguery that has paralyzed Congress on energy and environmental issues.

Midway through the 1970's, Republican Senator John Chafee emerged as America's greatest environmental legislator. He entered the Senate in 1976 and retired in 1999. As minority leader of the newly formed Senate Committee on the Environment and Public Works, Chafee was in a key position to influence the future of the Environmental Renaissance. Chafee had a strong affinity for the natural environment. He educated himself in the sciences as the years progressed. Chafee became particularly knowledgeable with regard to wetlands, estuaries, and the oceans. He was a man of courage, independence, and deep loyalty to America; his military service in the Pacific during World War II was distinguished. Chafee drafted, sponsored, and promoted many environmental provisions, and had impeccable judgment and foresight with regard to global warming/climate change.

The 1970's environmental statutes were quite readable, coherent, and enforceable, although necessarily complex and lengthy by 1970's standards (a couple of hundred pages, not a thousand). Congress went beyond simply delegating to the U.S. Environmental Protection Agency the power to regulate pollution. Congress listed scores of specific chemicals for regulation and set guidelines for standard-setting. The economic impact of pollution controls on industry was a factor studied in agency development documents for the new regulations. That did not mean that large capital or operating costs automatically doomed a new regulation; it was a balancing process. Sometimes the environmental harm was so unacceptable that it required a complete ban on the use of a chemical, such as polychlorinated biphenyls (PCB's). Often the final EPA rule contained a mixture of in-plant process changes, the substitution of alternative materials, and the installation of control equipment.

In the 1970's industry trade associations, lawyers, and lobbyists were working in Washington, and they made their views known, but the difference was two-fold: a) the legislators were not pawns of the special interests and did not consider their votes up for sale, and b) the number of lobbyists and amounts of money flowing into politics and government were very much smaller.

The list of statutes enacted is impressive:

- 1969 - The National Environmental Policy Act
- 1970 - The Clean Air Act
- 1972 - The Clean Water Act, the Marine Mammal Protection Act, and the Coastal Zone Management Act
- 1973 - The Endangered Species Act
- 1974 and 1977 - The Safe Drinking Water Act
- 1976 - The Resource Conservation and Recovery Act (regulating all solid and hazardous waste) and The Toxic Substances Control Act
- 1980 - The Comprehensive Environmental Response, Compensation and Liability Act ("the Superfund Law") providing for a private/public clean-up of hazardous substances dumped at hundreds of locations around the country in years past

It was Republican president Richard M. Nixon who created the EPA and later the Council on Environmental Quality to advise the White House. Despite his conservative urge for tight control over domestic spending, Nixon fully funded the necessary expansions of the Justice Department and the other agencies and departments needed to implement the new laws. Environmental prosecutors in the Nixon administration enforced the laws—old and new. In the early stages the Justice Department filed civil enforcement actions under the federal common law of public nuisance and the *1899* Rivers and Harbors Act. It was the best legal authority that the Justice Department could muster at this point. Occasionally, corporate executives were summoned to grand juries. Those who doubted the will and competence of young Justice Department attorneys in a Republican administration had big surprises coming.

Nixon made strong appointments to new environmental posts: Russell Train and Bill Ruckleshaus at EPA, Nathaniel Reed at the Department of Fish and Wildlife, and others. Nixon was sensitive to the grass-roots environmental movements, including the well-established nonprofit groups, Ducks Unlimited, Trout Unlimited, the National Wildlife Federation, and the Conservation Foundation. The Republican Party was filled with sportsmen, lovers of the out-of-doors, and members of these nonprofits. More wetlands conservation took place through these organizations than all of the other programs combined.

The Environmental Renaissance ended in 1980, but it set the stage for major accomplishments afterwards with acid rain and the ozone hole (see Chapter 8) and the Oil Pollution Act of 1990 that Chafee promoted—a major upgrade of federal law governing oil pollution. Chafee continued to educate himself on the remaining man-made assaults on the environment. He analyzed them with intelligence and integrity—and the farsightedness of Theodore Roosevelt. Chafee left his mark with what he championed and lost as well as with his successes. There were two issues in the former category: America's petroleum addiction and America's emission of greenhouse gases causing global warming/climate change.

The updated statistics on the petroleum addiction that Chafee tried to reverse decades ago are astounding. The U.S. Department of Energy and Energy Information Administration project (as of April 2016) that America will consume in 2016 an average of *387 million gallons of motor gasoline every day.*[7] The per-capita consumption of petroleum products by Americans is grossly disproportionate to that in other countries (twice that in Germany, for example). The DOE issues a weekly report on crude oil production and import. In the week ended April 22, 2016, America imported 7.6 million barrels (a barrel is 42 gallons) of crude oil and produced domestically 8.9 million barrels. Thus, even though America now exports some fossil fuels, it is more than *40% reliant on imports.*[8] Americans' dependence on unstable and occasionally hostile countries for a huge amount of the petroleum that we consume poses an ongoing threat to U.S. national security. Furthermore, the extraction, transportation, refining, and combustion of this product generate huge amounts of pollution in many forms to air, water, and land.

Chafee proposed a Gas-Guzzler Tax on the sale of automobiles that squandered fuel. Congress gutted the Gas-Guzzler bill by *exempting* the most rapidly rising class of new vehicles at the time, Sport Utility Vehicles, along with the most inefficient vehicles, trucks.

Chafee strongly supported mass transportation. While America built more and more cars, trucks, and roads, and ignored the advantages of rail transportation[9], Europe and Asia were developing fast, modern rail systems that promoted more efficient commerce and a cleaner environment. America was willfully losing its edge. Some of America's turnpikes have now become so clogged with trucks that they look more like tractor-trailer parking lots than thoroughfares. Meanwhile, the rail system of the Northeast Corridor lies nearby.

The Arab Oil Embargo in 1973 was sufficient incentive for Congress to enact the first fuel-economy standards for passenger cars in miles per gallon (mpg); there was an immediate positive impact. But the vehicle-mpg curve *flat-lined* in the 1980's as the Neoconservative political wave swept over Washington. Annual visits to Capitol Hill by domestic CEO's for Congressional hearings on these standards produced a stream of misrepresentations from the industry, i.e., that it was not economically or technologically feasible to manufacture and sell fuel-efficient vehicles. European and Asian companies were already putting the lie to this testimony.

The original eight-cylinder gas-guzzlers of the 1970's "achieved" approximately 14 miles per gallon. The official 2015 Fuel Economy Guide[10] shows that current models of SUV's and pick-up trucks still achieve only 13-17 mpg off the highway (which is a large percentage of the time, especially for SUV's) and 17-24 mpg on the highway. Moreover, EPA itself admits that these mpg estimates overstate fuel economy in actual driving, particularly in winter when engine efficiency declines. Most experts place the error at 15% of the mpg. Applying that adjustment, we can see that, particularly with the huge shift away from cars and toward SUV's and light trucks, America remains a severe oil glutton, and this gluttony detracts from the nation's credibility in making a formal pledge to reduce greenhouse gases at the 21st Century Conference of Parties (COP) in Paris in December 2015.[11] The agreement, discussed later, is known as the "Paris Accord."

The precipitous fall in oil and gas prices (a gallon of regular gasoline costs approximately $2.00 at the time of writing) has exacerbated the national oil addiction. The transportation sector is responsible for a quarter of all the petroleum consumed in the U.S. and a quarter of greenhouse gases emitted. Motor vehicles are by far the least efficient users of petroleum products (the combustion engine is only 21% efficient).[12] As of December 1, 2015, the Wall Street Journal Market Data Center reported a year-to-date *decrease* in small car sales (-1.6%) compared to a 16.8% increase in luxury SUV sales and a 12.5% increase in Light Duty Vehicles, including Pick-ups, SUV's, SUV/Crossovers, and minivans.[13] The data confirm that gasoline price is a determining factor in consumers' choices of vehicle. In a country with huge metropolitan areas, *none* of the top three best-selling vehicles in America is a car.

When gas prices approached $4.00 per gallon a few years ago, consumers reacted. It appears to be the "conservation price" that must be maintained (or close to it) by gas taxes in order to change Americans' undisciplined ways. It can no longer be argued that there is not a wide selection of good-quality, fuel-efficient models being produced. By forcing conservation through the tax, European nations have altered public habits and fashions. Europe and Japan have more fuel-efficient passenger vehicles and ultra-modern rail systems that benefit businesses and the people. American oil and highway lobbies and their allies have always argued that more expensive gasoline throws the country into an economic recession, whereas cheap gas brings economic growth, jobs, and the people's economic well-being. The last five years have thoroughly destroyed this propaganda. Gas prices were not the determining factor on economic health either on the way up or the way down, as economists now admit. The precipitous drop in price has clearly *not* spurred the economic growth claimed.[14] The President of the San Francisco Federal Reserve Board, John C. Williams, said bluntly: "We got this wrong."[15]

In 1990, *twenty-five years ago,* John Chafee gave a landmark speech on the floor of the Senate stating that 49 Nobel laureates and 700 members of the National Academy of Sciences had accepted the thesis of man-induced global warming and the remaining question was how to reduce the emission of greenhouse gases.[16] He described how greenhouse gases (carbon dioxide, methane, and other substances) released at the earth's surface rise up to form an atmospheric layer that traps heat below. Chafee said:

> The testimony of scientific experts suggests that it is time for us to act on this problem… In fact, there is remarkable agreement that the threat from global warming is real. The debate is over the rate at which global warming is occurring… But those who argue for more study today are themselves out of step with the great preponderance of world scientific opinion.[17]

Chafee emphasized that the risk was not limited to wildlife and their habitat. He cited the risk to human beings living in coastal areas where there would be flooding. "Those are obviously real and very, very serious consequences," he said.

Chafee's pioneer global-warming speech on the floor of the Senate seems to have passed completely by an ignorant, dysfunctional, and corrupt body of lawmakers on Capitol Hill. Since then the evidence of the urgency of this threat has steadily mounted.

When the 1970's are viewed as a whole, however, Chafee's inability to sway Congress in the right direction on two major issues does not detract from the historic national achievement of overcoming multiple civic breakdowns and demonstrating through the Environmental Renaissance and the enactment of the Civil Rights laws that America had reinstated the "just administration of a good government."

---

[1] George Washington, *George Washington—Writings*, (New York: Literary Classics of the U.S., 1997), 766.

[2] Frank Rich, "The State of the Union is Comatose," NYT (hereafter "NYT"), 30 January 2010.

[3] United Nations Press Release SG/1749, "Secretary-General Signs Earth Day Proclamation," 26 February 1971; http://www.themesh.com/un.htm (24 February 2004).

[4] Thomas Rees, "Saving the environment through dialogue and transparency," *Francis: The Environment Encyclical*, 10 September 2015, National Catholic Reporter. http://www.ncronline.org.

[5] Brett Walton, "Voices from the Past: Nixon, Congress Debate the Clean Water Act," CircleofBlue.org, 11 October 2012. See also, James Annis, *Howard Baker: Conciliator in an Age of Crisis* (Lanham, MD: Madison Books, 1995).

---

⁶ This institution seems well suited to play a role in the democracy-reform process discussed below.

⁷ All data are published online by the U.S. Energy Information Administration, in this case in the "Short-Term Energy Outlook" and the "Weekly Petroleum Status Report Highlights". www.eia.gov.

⁸ EIA, "Weekly Petroleum Status Report Highlights, Summary for the Week ending April 22, 2016. www.eia.gov/petroleum/supply/weekly.

⁹ In April 2015, the EPA produced a report: *Inventory of U.S. Greenhouse Gas Emissions and Sinks: 1990-2003* and posted various supporting materials on its website. http://www3.epa.gov/climatechange/ghgemissions/usinventoryreport.html. Between 1990 and 2005, tractor-trailers became 12% *less* fuel-efficient (while railroads became 20% *more* efficient). This resulted from an increase in empty miles driven, small shipments, and engine-idling in increasingly congested corridors. Freight-truck greenhouse gas emissions *increased* 69% between 1990 and 2005. The statistics make an overwhelming argument for a crash rail development program in the U.S. even apart from the compelling economic advantages. The mindless 50-year pro-vehicle obsession certainly has the earmarks of one form of national suicide. The transportation sector accounts for more than a quarter of total GHG emissions. Trucks carry 70% of the nation's freight— the *inverse* of ratios in other countries around the world where energy conservation and labor productivity are top priorities. The U.S. emits approximately a quarter of the world's estimated greenhouse gases, second only to China. The "energy intensity" (BTU's/ton-mile) of freight hauled by truck is almost ten times that of freight hauled by rail according to the Inventory. The Association of American Railroads estimates that rail carriers haul a ton of freight 469 miles on *one* gallon of fuel, and if only 10% of long-distance freight switched from road to rail, we would save one billion gallons of fuel per year and 12 million tons of GHG's emitted.

¹⁰ http://www.fueleconomy.gov.

¹¹ Lynne Peeples, "Historic Climate Change Agreement Adopted in Paris," The Huffington Post, 12 December 2015. www.huffingtonpost.com.

¹² U.S. Energy Information Administration data (2011) cited in Jonathan Shaw, "Altering Course: Why the United States may be on the cusp of an energy revolution," Harvard Magazine, May–June 2015, 49.

¹³ Wall Street Journal Market Data Center, citing www.motorintelligence.com, 1 December 2015. http://online.wsj.com.

¹⁴ Binyamin Applebaum, "This Time, Cheaper Oil Does Little for the U.S. Economy," NYTimes.com, Today's Headlines, 22 January 2016.

¹⁵ Id.

¹⁶ Congressional Record, S13059ff, 13 September 1990, Debate on the Motor Vehicle Fuel Efficiency Act; http://www.thomas.loc.gov.

¹⁷ Id.

Chapter 7

Demagoguery

"How frequently too will the honest but unenlightened leader be the dupe [fool] of a favorite leader, veiling his selfish views under the professions of public good, and varnishing his sophistical arguments with the glowing colours of popular eloquence?"
—*James Madison, Vices of the Political System (1787)*[1]

Although James Madison does not use the word "demagoguery" in this excerpt from *Vices,* he effectively gives us an ornate definition of this word. Because of Madison's unique status, we should pay particular attention to it. That it came about in 1787 is, once again, extraordinary.

Demagoguery is derived from two Greek roots that mean "the people" (as in "democracy") and "to lead," i.e., leading the people. The particular type of leadership meant by this word is not good. It is a leader's corrupt, self-seeking manipulation of the people for his or her own personal or partisan gain. A demagogue is a political or other type of leader who exploits their position of power and the ignorance of the audience by making false or exaggerated claims, promises, or attacks and through fear-mongering and appealing to racial, ethnic, and other prejudices. The tools of the demagogue are his or her words.

It will become clear, if it has not already, why I devote two chapters of the book to demagoguery.

Madison, like Washington, abhorred the possibility that America might by ripped apart by factions based on political views, money and greed, or social status. Demagoguery is one aspect of factionalism. In Madison's illustration, the demagogue is a "favorite leader" who professes to be promoting the public good when his real motivation is his own advancement, and who is an expert at manipulating others with high-sounding language. He "varnishes his sophistical arguments with the glowing colours of popular eloquence." Sophistry is false reasoning made to look correct through the artifice of flowery language and appeals to passion. In Madison's scenario the victim of the demagogue is not fundamentally dishonest or ignorant; he is

61

unenlightened—lacking critical knowledge and judgment—and, unfortunately, that lack is a fatal flaw in any person in high public or private office. Thus, the victim is vulnerable to demagoguery because of his ignorance, not his vice, and many Americans today find themselves in the same position.

One of America's most plain-spoken presidents was Democrat Harry S. Truman of Missouri, who was propelled into the Oval Office by the death of President Franklin Roosevelt during World War II. Truman is known for his empathy with the common man, his humility, and his life-long passion for history. Truman is said to have "internalized" history.[2] When a problem or crisis arose, he did what Jefferson had counseled—he reflexively drew upon his knowledge of the Founders, American history, and the history of other republics that met unhappy ends. He considered the big picture and the core principles of America.

One writer has listed "Harry Truman's History Lessons."[3] Truman's first lesson was that republics are fragile for precisely the reasons we have been discussing. His second lesson was that democratic government "has a moral basis."[4] This is not true with respect to other forms of government. A democratic leader must choose what is good, not follow personal or public whims. Truman understood that good leadership is not a popularity contest and that a demagogue who plays to the people with his "varnished" sophistry is causing the worst harm to the republic. Truman, like Madison and Theodore Roosevelt, made known his deep suspicion of demagogues.[5]

According to the Truman profile written by Samuel W. Rushay, Jr. for the National Archives' online magazine, *Prologue,* Truman cited the case of the Athenian Aristides, who was honorable, and yet was banished by the people because he did not play up to them, while Alcibiades was favored even though he was a "first class demagogue."[6] Truman declared that a good education in history is critical for the youth, that each generation must learn the lessons of history for itself, and that *every citizen owes public service to the government.* If young people do not understand and appreciate what they have, Truman said, "it will go the way of the... city states of Greece, the great Roman Republic and the Dutch Republic."[7] "Individuals matter," Truman was fond of saying.

More recently, author Cullen Murphy wrote a book entitled *Are We Rome? The Fall of an Empire and the Fate of America.*[8] The title of this 2007 book raised the right question, but neither Murphy nor the National Constitution Center that presented a special exhibition of the same name presented a deep analysis of the issue for Americans. They seemed to believe that the social and cultural distinctions between Rome and twenty-first century America grant America some sort of immunity to civic collapse. One wonders whether, if Mr. Cullen had listened to the 2016 Republican presidential campaign, he would have modified his optimistic outlook regarding the potential for this republic to collapse. It is not necessary to have blood on the floor of the rotunda for a republic to collapse.

Republican Senator Joe McCarthy of Wisconsin was America's archetypal demagogue during the 1950's. Most Americans today know little of McCarthyism, the workings of demagoguery, and their relevance today. McCarthy chose a platform that was convenient at the time: fear of Communism. He became Chairman of the Senate Permanent Subcommittee on Investigations and worked in tandem with the House Un-American Activities Committee. The two Committees launched a virulent campaign against American citizens suspected of being "Communist sympathizers" and "subversives." The victims included a wide range of intellectuals, artists and writers, "liberals," persons affiliated with the entertainment industry, Jews, legal immigrants, suspected homosexuals, employees of the U.S. Departments of State and the Army—and persons having *some connection* to any of the above. Many citizens lost their jobs, were posted on the newly developed Hollywood Blacklist, and had their reputations smeared.

In retrospect, McCarthy's basic tool-chest of lies, innuendoes, insinuations, prejudices, bullying, and fear-mongering seems too outrageous to have captured the minds of such a large segment of America for so long. McCarthyism permeated Congress, the Republican Party, and the daily newspapers for years. Three individuals deserve most credit for finally taking McCarthy down: CBS news broadcaster Edward R. Murrow,[9] Boston trial attorney Joseph Welch, representing the Department of the Army in the Congressional Army-McCarthy hearings (the first televised and radio-broadcasted committee hearings), and Republican Senator Margaret Chase Smith of Maine, whose role is much less well known.

Senator Smith was deeply loyal to America. She had a legendary record of attendance at voting roll calls; reportedly, she never missed a roll call on a bill in thirteen years. She had been watching her Republican Party—and the whole Senate—being disgraced by McCarthy's witch-hunt. Rather than remaining mute and allowing partisan politics to control her actions (which is the current order of the day on Capitol Hill), in June 1950 Senator Smith went to the floor of the Senate and delivered a "Declaration of Conscience" reminiscent of the pamphlets and speeches of the Revolutionary War patriots.

In her Declaration, Senator Smith portrayed the desperate condition of America. She described:

> ... a national feeling of fear and frustration that could result in *national suicide* and the end of everything that we Americans hold dear. It is a condition that comes from lack of effective leadership in either the Legislative Branch or the Executive Branch of our Government.[10]

She proceeded:

> I think it is high time that we remember that we have sworn to uphold and defend the Constitution... I am not proud of the way in which the Senate has been made a publicity platform for irresponsible sensationalism... I don't like the way the Senate has been made a *rendez-vous* for vilification, for selfish political gain at the sacrifice of individual reputations and national unity.

Her words resonate in twenty-first-century ears—especially the phrase "national suicide" that seems particularly descriptive of the downward spiral since the 1980's.

Senator Smith proposed the appointment of an advisory commission to lead Congress and the country out of the swamp that McCarthy had created. It was a bold move on her part to suggest that the United States Senate had become so infected that it was unable to reform itself or the country, and that an advisory commission was needed. This is a recommendation we should keep in mind.

Later, Senator Smith, recognizing the direction in which the Republican Party was being pulled, offered herself as an independent candidate for the presidency as an alternative to the Conservative Republican, Barry Goldwater. She was following in the steps of Theodore Roosevelt, a man who would have single-handedly pulverized McCarthyism.

Another shameful episode of demagoguery in America involved a pre-World War II group—the Isolationists. From September 1939, when Hitler invaded Poland, until December 1941, when Japan bombed America into the war, an Isolationist Movement conducted a successful demagogic campaign to block this country from coming to the rescue of Britain and the Allies. Britain, of course, was America's strongest ally and, after France fell, it was the last great bastion of democracy and freedom. The Nazis rampaged through Europe from Poland to France; there was no doubt regarding Hitler's fascist objectives, his demonic obsessions, and his military capability. Spain and Italy had fallen to fascists—Franco and Mussolini, respectively.

There was also no doubt that Britain had an extraordinary Prime Minister, Winston Churchill, who was profoundly committed to virtually the same fundamental principles as those of the Founders (although he did have some attachment to the old British Empire). During the course of *twenty-six months* of American Isolationism Churchill poured forth telegrams, letters, and speeches that were more authentically American—more in tune with the Founders—than anything spoken or heard on this side of the Atlantic.

Churchill made a daring voyage by ship to meet and negotiate with President Franklin Roosevelt off Newfoundland. He was constantly applying his considerable intellect, charm, wit, and eloquence to persuade FDR to come to the aid of Britain. He kept Roosevelt up to date on the war; he reported, correctly at the time, that Hitler's high command had plans on the table for a cross-channel invasion of Britain. German bombers were making nightly raids over London ("the Blitz") and destroying civilian buildings and killing innocent civilians. Hitler's aim was to demoralize the people and force them to surrender to the Third Reich. Churchill pleaded for the United

States to enter the war and join the Allies. He was desperate for war materiel and was willing to accept contributions of musty World War I ships and guns, but Congress had passed the Neutrality Acts as a reaction to the insanity of a very different war, World War I. These acts forbade the supply of armaments to any allies engaged in any war unless purchases were cash-and-carry; that placed an enormous financial burden on the much smaller nation. One of the best accounts of the period is Jon Meacham's *Franklin and Winston*.[11] Although Americans had reason to want to avoid another world war, it was no more than a pipe dream. Hitler left no doubts as to his intention for global fascist domination and for the elimination of any races, ethnic groups, or intellectual ideas that he deemed a threat to his mission of Aryan supremacy.

Churchill began to win FDR's sympathy. One of FDR's top aides, Harry Hopkins, spent considerable time with Winston in London and reported back to FDR the merits of Winston's case. Meacham tells the story of Churchill's boundless energy and his late-night brainstorming sessions that left Hopkins completely awed by the vigor, determination, and high principles of this man. FDR did increase sales to the Allies, but the difference between Churchill and FDR was that FDR was a serious public-poll watcher. A strong majority of Americans, under the influence of the Isolationists, opposed coming to Britain's aid *even if the Nazis did invade*. Demagoguery had rarely achieved such heights.

U.S. Army Chief of Staff George C. Marshall may not have qualified as an Isolationist, but he opposed sending war materiel to the Allies because, notwithstanding everything Churchill said and did and that Hopkins (and FDR) knew to be true regarding the man, Marshall thought Britain would surrender and allow the arms to fall into German hands.[12] Then there were the real Isolationists—that assortment of wealthy businessmen, senators, German sympathizers, and public figures like Charles Lindberg. Their front organization was the America First Committee. Lindberg's most memorable derogatory speech was given as late as September 11, 1941, when the horror of the Nazis was well enough known to have put an immediate end to Isolationism. In this speech Lindberg pointed the finger at the British, the FDR administration, and the Jews as warmongers.[13] The worst part was that these Isolationists did not even hope for an Allied victory against Hitler; they predicted Germany's victory and concluded that America, by refusing to engage, would be left standing as Hitler's most opportune trading partner. Civilizations would be destroyed and the Founders' principles would be trampled, but Americans might become *richer*.

The Isolationist Movement had not weakened even in May–June 1940 when Americans watched newsreels of the Nazis forcing the Allies back into a small corner of France (Dunkirk) with their backs to the channel. The British launched an incredible armada of civilian and military boats and vessels of all descriptions; they crossed over from England to rescue more than 300,000 troops in eleven days. It was a feat of civilian and military heroism and ingenuity unmatched. Obviously, it did not move the Isolationists or their sympathizers

In January 1941 Lindberg declared that there should be a negotiated peace with Hitler, an absurd and horrid proposition.

Knowing that the British could not afford to purchase the necessary war materiel, FDR went ahead and signed an agreement in September 1940 to hand over fifty outdated destroyers to the Royal Navy in return for leases of properties under British control. FDR sparked a movement for the passage of the Lend-Lease Act that drew considerable opposition, especially from Republicans. Lindberg testified against the bill. In March 1941 the Act finally passed; America would receive long-term leases for bases in British colonial islands in the Caribbean, Newfoundland, and elsewhere.

Japan finally bombed America into the war in December 1941.

Demagoguery, of course, is not unique to America. However, it is a particular threat in democratic republics where there is free speech and the people are vested with ultimate political power. The Internet and burgeoning infotainment industry have played a major role in the resurgence of demagoguery. Aristotle and Rousseau, the Founders and Theodore Roosevelt, Murrow and Senator Smith all agreed that a large democratic republic is especially vulnerable to this type of disease. Instead of being on the alert against demagogues, however, Americans, ignorant of history and civics and bereft of journalists like Murrow and legislators like Smith, have become victims of a much larger and more dangerous wave of demagoguery.

[1] *Vices*, Sec.11, 1.

[2] Samuel W. Rushay, Jr., "Harry Truman's History Lessons," *Prologue Magazine,* The National Archives, Spring 2009, vol. 49, no. 1.

[3] Id.

[4] Id (not paginated).

[5] Id.

[6] Id.

[7] Id.

[8] Cullen Murphy, *Are We Rome? The fall of an Empire and the Fate of America* (Boston: Houghton Mifflin, 2007).

[9] Murrow's story is portrayed well in a movie entitled *Good Night and Good Luck.*

[10] Margaret Chase Smith, "A Declaration of Conscience" (1 June 1950), collected in *American Rhetoric—Top 100 Speeches* (italics mine). http://www.americanrhetoric.com/speeches/margaretchasesmithconscience.html.

[11] Jon Meacham, *Franklin and Winston—An Intimate Portrait of an Epic Friendship* (New York: Random House, 2003).

[12] U.S. Department of State Office of the Historian, "Milestone: 1937-1945—Lend-Lease and Military Aid to the Allies in the Early Years of World War II," accessed 17 December 2015. https://history.state.gov/milesyones/1937-1945/lend-lease.

[13] Meacham, 54–55, 95, 127.

Chapter 8

The New Age of Demagoguery

The hole in the stratospheric ozone layer that protects the earth from solar radiation "never existed"; banning chlorofluorocarbons ("CFC's") by Act of Congress (pursuant to international protocol signed by the U.S.) was an "act of environmental panic"; the earth's atmosphere is growing cooler, not warmer, and any increases in temperature might have a "beneficial effect"; anthropogenic global warming is "the greatest hoax ever perpetrated on the American people"; and "the global warming movement has completely collapsed."
—*Quotations from the U.S. Senate Internet website of Ranking Minority Member Republican James N. Inhofe, Committee on the Environment and Public Works (2011-12)*

In the post-1980 period America entered a new age of demagoguery. This demagoguery in some ways resembles McCarthyism. A faction forms around a central ideology, the members of the faction broadcast their views with arrogance, they abuse and intimidate people with slurs and misrepresentations, they exploit their public position, and they refuse to waver regardless of the truth and the character of their victims. The new demagogues went further. They defied a definitive judicial ruling of the United States Supreme Court in 2007 that acknowledged the gravity of global warming/climate change and ordered the Environmental Protection Agency under President George W. Bush to regulate the emission of greenhouse gases as air pollutants under the Clean Air Act.

The anti-global-warming cult is the principal illustration of the new demagoguery in this chapter. However, it is in the nature of the demagogues that they rotate from one issue to another using the same tactics, never acknowledging wrong, and always seeking public acclaim and personal aggrandizement—at the expense of the republic. Demagogues do not quit; they never apologize; and they never reform.

A New York Times columnist, David Brooks, has described the new era not explicitly in terms of demagoguery but of seduction and deception. Brooks titled his May 2012 article, tongue in cheek, "The Age of Innocence."[1] People have been seduced into believing that enforcing accountability is old school. Leaders "do not believe that their job is to restrain popular will" but rather "to flatter and satisfy it," Brooks said. The flawed concept is that there are no absolutes, no fundamental principles, and no innate tendencies toward human vice rather than virtue that must be restrained. This shift in thinking leaves society highly vulnerable to demagoguery. As Brooks said, "A giant polling apparatus has developed to help leaders anticipate and respond to popular whims." Considering that this status is the complete opposite of the moral and civic imperative that Harry Truman and others tried to instill in Americans, a good response might be to select Truman's and Roosevelt's lessons for the program "One City—(or State or Country)—One Book."

Brooks concludes that there is no prospect of rehabilitation until "we rediscover and acknowledge our own natural weaknesses and learn to police rather than lionize [idolize] our own impulses."

How far do these impulses go? The chapters that follow on disease in industry and disease in Congress provide some answers. In the 2016 election cycle, fact-checkers were unable to keep pace with the lies and misrepresentations spewed out by candidates for the Office of the President of the United States. In one case, repeated lying about the candidate's prior experience, when exposed, still did not end his candidacy.[2] The Republican nominee, a casino, real estate, television, and business billionaire, Donald Trump, has denied global warming/climate change since 2012 in much the same language as used by elected president George W. Bush; former Republican nominee, Mitt Romney; former vice president aspirant Sarah Palin; and former Senate Environment Committee minority leader James Inhofe. The latest article on Trump's climate-change denial, as of May 30, 2016, refers to his 2012 Twitter comment that the concept of global warming was created by and for the Chinese to make U.S. manufacturing non-competitive.[3]

This behavior is classic demagoguery. There was no China plot—and could be none. The U.S. and China both signed the 2015 Paris Accord discussed below that would reduce global average temperature to not greater than 1.5 degrees Celsius above pre-industrial levels. (The Accord is known as "COP21," i.e., the 21st Session of the United Nations Framework Convention on Climate Change.) Both countries, along with 193 others, sent delegates to Bonn in May 2016 to commence implementation while formal ratification of the Accord proceeds.[4]

We are jumping ahead of ourselves. When he published his U.S. Senate Internet website in 2011–12 (excerpted above) Republican Senator James N. Inhofe held the same position that Republican Senator John Chafee had previously held, Ranking Minority Member of the Committee on the Environment and Public Works. He was the nation's second highest environmental legislator. Republicans even considered giving him the chairmanship in 2015. Inhofe flippantly denied the existence of environmental phenomena that were scientifically well proven and of the highest strategic importance to the entire world. Global-warming/climate change was actually America's third encounter with trans-boundary atmospheric pollution. The first two encounters were with acid rain and ozone-destroying chlorofluorocarbons (CFC's). It is worthwhile comparing how the three different phenomena were handled politically and legally in the United States.

Acid rain is caused primarily by emission into the air of sulfur dioxide (SO_2) that, in turn, combines with precipitation and falls to the earth as dilute sulfuric acid. Observable effects are the erosion of stone structures and the acidification of lakes and ponds, especially at high elevations. Trout and other aquatic organisms were completely eliminated from otherwise pristine water bodies, for example, in the Adirondack Mountains in the United States and the Laurentian Mountains in Quebec Province, Canada. The main sources of the SO_2 were the electric-power generating facilities located upwind from the water bodies—in Pennsylvania, the Midwest, and Canada. While the pollution was not visible to the naked eye of a person on the ground, scientists, engineers, and climatologists had no difficulty establishing the sources, the transport, and the lake acidification. If we deny what we cannot observe with the naked eye, then we are taking a huge leap backward in civilization to medieval times before Galileo. This we cannot do.

There are many men and women who love the out-of-doors, many sportsmen who enjoy the environment, and many persons who appreciate—or even are memorialized by—stone monuments and sculpture, art, and so forth. Trout Unlimited and Ducks Unlimited were formed long ago by the first two categories; they have always been broad-based, grass-roots organizations, and they included many Republicans. While the large electric-power generating companies initially fought attempts to require the installation of expensive SO_2 scrubbers or the use of more expensive low-sulfur coal, the truth was clear, and members of both political parties in Congress and the White House did not allow the skirmish to last long.

In 1990 Congress enacted a new subchapter of the Clean Air Act requiring industry to remove massive amounts of SO_2 from their stack gases with scrubbers or through the use of low-sulfur coal. Scrubbers did cost a lot of money, but threats of huge economic dislocation were ill-founded. The plants were modernized and retrofitted. Costs were passed along to the consumers, who paid their bills.

America's second encounter with transboundary pollution was with the emission of CFC's and the depletion of the ozone layer. CFC's rise through the earth's atmosphere and the troposphere into the stratosphere where there is a layer of ozone that protects the earth from intense UV-B radiation from the sun. This radiation is extremely harmful to humans (causing skin cancers) and also to plants and aquatic organisms that are essential for the production of oxygen and life on earth. In 1984 British and Japanese scientists discovered a hole in the ozone layer above Antarctic pole.[5] The British discovery was reported in a journal in 1985. There was intense and rapid publicity—and follow-up here and abroad. In four years the United States became one of almost 200 countries signing the 1989 Montreal Protocol banning CFC's.

Only a few domestic industrial facilities manufactured, handled, or emitted ozone-destroying CFC's (a few other chemicals are also culprits). However, numerous pieces of equipment operating in the field with CFC's as refrigerants needed to be retrofitted or retired. The chemical phase-out and retrofitting process is still underway. Satellite imagery obtained regularly by NASA shows the presence of holes in the ozone layer located over the poles. The imagery does not lie.

Congress listened to the scientists and enacted another amendment to the Clean Air Act to phase out CFC's. The worldwide response to the ozone crisis is considered a model in international environmental diplomacy and regulation.

The ozone hole is still a very serious threat. It will continue to fluctuate seasonally for years as it slowly diminishes in size. The images are presented online, along with the latest discoveries.[6] The most recent discovery is a West Pacific/Southeast Asia hole that is allowing methane and CFC's to rise through the OH [hydroxyl radical] Shield in the troposphere. This is an alarming development because the hole facilitates the upward migration of a rapidly increasing load of pollutants from developing nations in that part of the world.

The Internet website rant of Inhofe set forth above constituted demagoguery of a larger order than McCarthyism because the victims were not particular individuals, but *all* humans, life forms, and ecosystems subjected to acid rain and solar radiation.

We now come to greenhouse gases ("GHG's") and global warming/climate change.

The science of global warming and climate change is well understood. The term "global warming" is not incorrect, but it is incomplete. All regions of the earth do not suffer the same type of environmental impacts from GHG's. Some areas experience extreme heat, drought, and wildfires; others have periodic, torrential rains and severe flooding. Overall, temperatures on or near the earth's surface are definitely increasing as a result of massive releases of carbon dioxide (CO_2) and other GHG's, but the most accurate term is climate change. Compared to acid rain and CFC's, the body of scientific data supporting anthropogenic (man-induced) climate change is now much larger and more diverse. As Senator John Chafee said in 1990, it is not a question any longer of whether or how climate change occurs, but of how to develop and implement effective, worldwide action programs.

CO_2 is the largest component of GHG's, and there are many fossil-fuel (mainly, petroleum products and coal) combustion sources of it, stationary and mobile. Methane is actually twenty-six times more potent than CO_2 in forming GHG's. It is released from household trash decomposing in landfills, wastewater treatment plants handling human waste, farm animal operations, oil and gas recovery operations, refineries, pipelines, and other sources. Ongoing sampling indicates that EPA may have underestimated methane emissions by a large percentage. When these new findings became known, Congress promptly responded to the agriculture lobby by preventing EPA from quantifying releases from animal farms and regulating them. Fortunately, there are nonpartisan, nonprofit associations now leading a movement for sustainable agriculture, but progress would be much swifter if government and industry at all levels could simply come together, agree on the negative causes and effects, and move ahead with remedial measures.[7] In September 2015, Mark Bittman, the well-known food editor of the Times, spoke to these priorities when he said he was shifting his efforts from cuisine alone to food and sustainable agriculture. Hopefully, there will be more crossover between these two vibrant areas: sustainable food/cuisine and sustainable agriculture.

The amount of CO_2 released to the stratosphere is substantially affected by deforestation. Trees and plants capture CO_2 as part of photosynthesis and oxygen production. A frenzy of deforestation has been occurring in the neotropical and tropical zones in Africa, Madagascar, Brazil, Mexico, Indonesia, and elsewhere. A recent televised documentary showed country-wide burning of forests in Indonesia, mainly to reap short-term rewards from palm oil production. This burning is estimated to generate a total amount of GHG's equal to the entire contribution of the United States.

CO_2 is captured by marine phytoplankton as well as trees. There are two types of microscopic plankton in the ocean (that feed baleen whales): phytoplankton (tiny plants) and zooplankton (tiny animals). The complex marine system known as the biological pump consists of latitudinal (north-south) temperature gradients that drive trade winds, which, in turn, drive cold-water upwellings from the depths to the surface, bringing masses of nutrients to feed marine algae. With climate change, the latitudinal temperature gradients are diminishing.[8] Phytoplankton produce *a quarter of the oxygen we breathe* (some sources say it is closer to 40%) and fix as much carbon as an entire forest; they also feed the organisms that are at the base of the food chain for all the fish in the ocean. Losing plankton is catastrophic. Four negative phenomena are interacting: the warming from greenhouse gas emissions emitted by human activities (including methane from livestock on cleared land), deforestation, direct pollution and destruction of the marine environment, and acidification of the oceans through carbonic acid rain.[9]

CO_2 and other gases form a greenhouse layer that permits solar radiation to penetrate down to the earth's surface but retards the release back of infrared radiation. The scientific evidence of anthropogenic releases of greenhouse gases and global warming has been accumulating at an accelerating rate across the globe for decades. Former Vice President Albert Gore published his book sixteen years after Chafee's speech.[10] There have been rising temperatures measured in the air and the oceans; glacial ice cores showing lower levels of CO_2 present before the huge increase in industrial activity; countless images showing receding ice fields from pole to pole; decades of U.S. Navy measurements of the thinning of polar ice in the Arctic (presenting a U.S. national security threat from the north and a huge threat to the oceans directly from exploitation of natural resources); significant increases in extreme weather events, including tornadoes, tropical downpours in the northeast, assaults of heat, drought, and wildfire; and outbreaks of invasive species thriving on warmer conditions. Pine-bark beetles have added a second reproduction cycle and have destroyed millions of acres of valuable forest and natural habitat in the Americas.[11]

Global warming is insidious because it sets off chain reactions. As snow, ice-cover, and permafrost melt, dark earth is exposed, more solar radiation is absorbed than reflected, methane from the exposed organic soils is released, and the process accelerates.[12] Many technical papers are collected online by the Intergovernmental Panel on Climate Change ("IPCC"), a leading international scientific body established by the United Nations and by C2ES: The Center for Climate and Energy Solutions (formerly the Pew Center on Climate Change).[13] In September 2013 the IPCC updated its assessment by the world's scientists. The IPCC said that human activity is the dominant cause of climate change, that many negative impacts are *well underway*, and that multiple lines of evidence support these assertions.[14]

If America had been the same nation that it was even in 1990 when the acid-rain Clean Air Amendments were enacted, we would have seen a different set of responses to climate change, but demagoguery, ignorance, and infotainment have eclipsed reason and responsibility.

George Shultz was one of the most highly regarded Republican statesmen of the last half century; he served under three Republican administrations as Secretary of the Departments of the Treasury, Labor, and State, and as Director of the Office of Management and the Budget (OMB). Shultz's reputation for sharp thinking and straight talking has grown over the years. Even in his eighties, Schultz devoted himself to promoting an energy policy that reduces our consumption of fossil fuels emitting CO_2. He has cited three compelling motivations: protecting national security, attacking pollution and global warming/climate change, and protecting the U.S. economy.[15]

Shultz has had a particular interest in the U.S. Navy's long-term monitoring of the Arctic Sea ice. He opposed California Proposition 23 that would have suspended an ambitious state law to curb greenhouse gases. He promoted a federal carbon tax that is revenue-neutral, i.e., he would give back to the citizens the revenue from the tax, a practice used by British Columbia. Global warming is not a matter of opinion, but of fact, Shultz said. He cited the progress under Republican administrations against acid rain and CFC's. Shultz's comments should have gained major attention from the news media and the politicians— especially Republicans. They should have put an end to the cultist demagoguery on this subject. That did not happen. The merry-go-round of demagoguery continued to whirl.

The story of the 2007 Supreme Court decision reveals more. Article III of the United States Constitution vests in the U.S. Supreme Court the power and duty to establish the supreme law of the land, by which all Americans, including the President and Vice President, must abide. During their two terms in office former President George W. Bush and Vice President Richard Cheney repeatedly rejected the scientific findings of anthropogenic global-warming/climate-change and refused to direct or allow the Environmental Protection Agency to regulate greenhouse gases. The case of <u>Massachusetts v. EPA</u> arose when environmental groups, the Commonwealth of Massachusetts, and others sued EPA to declare illegal its intransigent refusal to regulate greenhouse gases under the Clean Air Act. The Supreme Court finally ruled on April 2, 2007. George W. Bush was still in office. In a well-reasoned decision, the Court rejected all of the arguments put forth by the anti-global-warming cult. The Court's syllabus of its decision is powerful:

> Based on respected scientific opinion that a well-documented rise in global temperatures and attendant climatological and environmental changes have resulted from a significant increase in the atmospheric concentration of "greenhouse gases", a group of private organizations petitioned the Environmental Protection Agency (EPA) to begin regulating the emissions of four such gases... EPA ultimately denied the petition...
>
> The harms associated with climate change are serious and well recognized... [G]lobal warming threatens, *inter alia,* a precipitate rise in sea levels, severe and irreversible changes to natural ecosystems, a significant reduction in winter snowpack with direct and important economic consequences, and increases in the spread of disease and the ferocity of weather events...
>
> If the scientific uncertainty is so profound that it precludes EPA from making a reasoned judgment, it must say so... Instead, EPA rejected the rulemaking petition based on impermissible considerations. Its action was therefore "arbitrary, capricious, or otherwise not in accordance with law".[16]

When the Supreme Court's decision in <u>Massachusetts v. EPA</u> was handed down in 2007, Bush had an immediate obligation as our president to retract his false and illegal anti-climate-change position. In a democracy, we expect and depend upon the chief executive to tell the truth and follow the law, especially after Watergate and the <u>Nixon</u> court decision forcing that president to release his Oval Office tapes. But Bush did neither. In 2011 he gave his blessing to Republican presidential candidate Mitt Romney to continue defying the Supreme Court. This behavior is despotism.

On the campaign trail, Romney promised to *reverse* Obama's actions taken to comply with the court ruling, including regulation of greenhouse gas emissions from vehicles and other sources.[17] In a presidential campaign year America's 24-hour-a-day news media missed entirely—or deliberately avoided—the significance of the court decision and the Bush-Romney antics. Romney also attacked Obama's Clean Air Act regulation of heavy-truck emissions, an action that was forty years overdue.

In 2009, a prominent newspaper columnist, George Will, wrote an opinion piece for the Washington Post. Will used to be known as provocative and conservative, but not profoundly ignorant or defiant of Supreme Court law. Will entitled his piece "Dark Green Doomsayers." He approached the global-warming issue with flippant, pseudo-intellectual arrogance. Not possessing scientific qualifications of his own, Will used bogus citations to support his contention that global warming was a hoax and that the amount of global sea ice in 1990 was equal to that in 1979. The Washington Post, the daily newspaper of America's capital city, could have, and should have, exercised the editorial judgment not to publish this rank demagoguery—especially because of the great importance of the climate-change issue. Instead, the Post opted for demagoguery, sensationalism, and sales.[18]

Two of the Post's staff reporters later wrote their own story demolishing Will's article. They stated that the "widely circulated reports by Washington Post columnist George Will that Arctic ice [had] not significantly declined since 1979" were untrue and contradicted by the scientific data. The definitive data and maps refuting Will's statements had been in the public domain for years.[19]

If there were any retractions or apologies issued by either the Post or Will, I did not find them.

As the climate-change evidence continued to mount, the cult *grew*. On December 9, 2009, in the same newspaper, the unsuccessful Republican candidate for Vice President of the United States, Sarah Palin (also bearing no scientific credentials of her own—and not seeming to care) denigrated the top scientists in the world who had documented global warming. She referred to them as "so-called scientists." Palin, relying on computer-hacked emails, charged that a leading Penn State climatologist (Michael Mann) had manipulated the data to mislead the public with regard to global warming. This charge, if proven, could have destroyed Mann's career.[20] Palin also demanded that the U.S. president boycott an international conference on climate change to be held in Copenhagen—an arrogant, irresponsible demand to make at a critical point in time. Palin obviously wanted to be seen as a leader of the political cult so popular in the infotainment industry. She, too, defied the Supreme Court ruling.

Palin's attack on Mann was completely refuted by an independent Penn State investigatory panel on July 2, 2010. A researcher at the National Center for Atmospheric Research in Colorado noted that the panel's results were "absolutely no surprise." He commented that there were more than sufficient data and reports to support the dramatic global-warming graph by Mann, and that there were also other independent scientific findings that supported the conclusion that human activities cause climate change. Another scientist (from Texas A&M) commented that even if Mann's graph had not been supported, the climate models have become "increasingly convincing" and "it's becoming harder to ignore the retreat of the glaciers and shrinkage of sea ice."[21]

Again, no retraction or apology by the Post or Palin was found. A staff reporter wrote a piece stating that ice sheets in both Greenland and in Antarctica were melting at a *faster* rate than previously estimated, based on NASA data.[22]

Curiously, the Post did run an article stating that eleven Republican politicians were making their names by attacking global warming but did not set the record straight based on the Supreme Court decision or the scientific evidence. A responsible journalistic follow-up to Will, Palin, and the others would have been to cite the April 2007 decision of the United States Supreme Court and the latest findings.

The number of such incidents in the press—and of full-fledged plagiarism and fictitious reporting—signals a dire collapse in the quality of news reporting in America. In December 2015 New York Times Public Editor Margaret Sullivan raised a "red alert" in response to two incidents of front-page-article false reporting and the use of anonymous sources.[23]

Meanwhile, the broadcast media has captured a larger share of daily reporting, and the behavior there has been worse. Consider the Glenn Beck incidents. Neoconservative Glenn Beck has had a syndicated radio and television show for Fox News. Beck verbally assaulted former Vice President Albert Gore by saying that in Gore's educational campaign against climate change he was using the "same tactics" as Hitler when he was collecting and exterminating the Jews, that Gore's education of youth was analogous to Hitler's indoctrination of the youth (through Hitler Youth) and the addiction of youth by drug dealers.[24] The Anti-Defamation League denounced the Beck tirade, and Jewish Funds for Justice sent an open letter to the *Wall Street Journal* calling upon Fox News to sanction (punish) Beck for using Nazi and Holocaust imagery in his public tirade (which, in another country, would have brought him prosecution for a crime).[25]

That there was not a huge popular backlash against Beck and Fox remains inconceivable in America. Beck's behavior has been tracked by one of a new group of organizations that focuses on the truth or falsehood of public statements, *Media Matters*.[26] It is appalling that the elite traditional press has still not reformed itself and taken the lead in the movement for bringing truth to the American people. Beck has continued to write and have his books published, heavily marketed by book sellers, and sent to public libraries for "education" of the public. Although Beck has since gone in different directions, he is clearly the same Beck.

In 2007 Hans Blix gave an interview in which he was asked what he thought was the world's greatest threat. Blix was the former Director General of the International Atomic Energy Agency and former Head of the U.N. Monitoring, Verification and Inspection Commission, who maintained—correctly—that Saddam Hussein possessed no weapons of mass destruction and had no weapons delivery system that could present a legitimate threat to U.S. national security. In the 2007 interview, Blix said the following:

To me the question of the environment is more ominous than that of peace and war. We will have regional conflicts and use of force, but world conflicts I do not believe will happen any longer. But the environment, that is a creeping danger. I'm more worried about global warming than I am of any major military conflict.[27]

The Paris Accord does not hold the status of a U.S. treaty approved by two-thirds vote of the Senate. Thus, it is not a legally binding instrument in this country. However, it does have the status of an international agreement negotiated at great length among the U.S., China, and the rest of the world under the auspices of the United Nations Framework Convention on Climate Change. The President of France, François Hollande, declared that "The decisive deal for the planet is here."[28] Only a rogue president of a signatory nation would turn his back on this accomplishment. The President of COP21 stated that Donald Trump's nomination would "dramatically threaten" the future course of action finally agreed upon by the world of nations.[29]

In addition to the now-existing frameworks for country implementation and reporting, there are pledges to assist smaller nations to reduce emissions. The diplomacy that preceded the accord, between the United States and China in particular and also between France and others were historic. One would have hoped and expected that the Paris Accord would have prompted a shift in attitude and behavior in the American people and their representatives. If this shift is happening, it is not apparent among Republicans. It should be noted that a coalition of the most sophisticated industrial manufacturers in the United States accepted the climate-change science and the need to curb greenhouse gas emissions *years ago* when there was proposed legislation, the Waxman-Markey bill, pending in Congress.

The current level of political arrogance is unprecedented. Interestingly, Thomas Jefferson appreciated the magnitude of this threat in *1801* and chose to highlight it in his First Inaugural Address, as follows:

> And let us reflect that, having banished from our land that religious intolerance under which mankind so long bled and suffered, we have yet gained little if we countenance a political intolerance as despotic, as wicked, and as capable of as bitter and bloody persecutions.[30]

Jefferson was comparing two evils, political intolerance and religious intolerance. Millions of people can relate to religious intolerance, and Jefferson knew that. He wanted to elevate political intolerance—the demagoguery and divisiveness that destroy republics—to the same level. Other great Americans have had the same aim, e.g., Washington, Madison, Adams, Theodore Roosevelt, Abraham Lincoln, and Margaret Chase Smith. The consequences of not heeding them are now before us.

---

[1] David Brooks, "The Age of Innocence," *NYT*, 18 May 2012. http://www.nytimes.com/2012/05/18/opinion/the-age-of-innocence.html.

[2] The most complete account of Presidential Candidate Ben Carson's public lies appears to be found in an article of the online Esquire Magazine. Robert Bateman, "Ben Carson Debunked: Inside His Made-Up West Point Story," 10 November 2015, esquire.com.

[3] Janet Redman, Institute for Policy Studies, "Trump's Climate Change Denial Is Already Complicating the Paris Climate Deal," 27 May 2016, Huffington Post. www.huffingtonpost.com/janet-redman.

[4] COP21. www.COP21.gouv.fr.

[5] The Ozone Hole, Inc., http://www.theozonehole.com. The Ozone Hole is a nonprofit group formed by the U.S. National Aeronautical and Atmospheric Administration (NASA), the British Antarctic Study, Environment Canada, and others; the executive director of the Ozone Hole is Charles Welch.

[6] Id.

[7] E.g., Pennsylvania Association for Sustainable Agriculture.

[8] www.genoscope.cns.fr; University of California at San Diego, "Climate Change–The Marine Carbon Cycle," http:earthguide.ucsd.edu.

[9] Oceanic Preservation Society and Discovery Channel, *Racing Extinction* (film), Louie Psihoyos, Dir. (2015); http://racingextinction.com.

[10] Albert Gore, *An Inconvenient Truth: The Planetary Emergency of Global Warming & What We Can Do About It* (New York: Rodale Books, 2006). A film documentary (*An Inconvenient Truth*) was produced by Paramount in 2006.

[11] Scott Weidensaul, *Return to Wild America* (New York: North Point Press, 2005), 314–319.

[12] Id.

[13] The Intergovernmental Panel on Climate Change; http://ipcc.ch/. C2ES: Center for Climate and Energy Solutions; http://www.c2ES.org/.

[14] IPCC Press Release. 27 September 2013. www.ipcc.ch/news; www.climatechange2013.org.

[15] Mark Golden and Mark Shwartz, "Stanford's George Shultz on energy: It's personal," Stanford Report, 12 July 2012.

[16] Supreme Court of the United States, <u>Massachusetts et al. v. Environmental Protection Agency et al.</u>, Syllabus, 2 April 2007.

[17] Brad Johnston, "Romney Pledges to Kill Existing Fuel Economy Standards," Climate Progress, 5 December 2011. http://thinkprogress.org/climate/2011/12/05/382001/romney. See also, U.S. EPA Office of Transportation and Air Quality, "EPA and NHTSA Set

Standards to Reduce Greenhouse Gases and Improve Fuel Economy for Model Year 2017–2025 Car and Light Trucks," EPA-42—F-12-051, August 2012. http://www.epa.gov/otaq.

[18] George Will, "Dark Green Doomsayers," *Washington Post*, 15 February 2009.

[19] Juliet Eilperin and Mary Beth Sheridan, "New Data Show Rapid Arctic Ice Decline," *Washington Post*, 7 April 7 2009, A3.

[20] Sarah Palin, "Sarah Palin on politicization of Copenhagen climate conference," *Washington Post,* 9 December 2009.

[21] Faye Flam, "Penn State panel clears climatologist Michael Mann in e-mail case," *Philadelphia Inquirer*, 2 July 2010.

[22] Brian Vastag, "Ice Sheets melting faster than earlier estimates," *Washington Post*, 9 March 2011.

[23] Kate Sarru, "NY Times Public Editor: Flawed Stories Should Be 'Red Alert' for Paper," Media Matters for America; http://mediamatters.org/blog/2015/12/18.

[24] Media Matters Staff, "Glenn Beck's History of Using the Holocaust to Advance His Political Agenda," Media Matters, 22 August 2011; http://mediamatters.org/research/2011/08/22. Andrew Ironside, "Beck said Gore using 'same tactic' in fight against global warming as Hitler did against Jews," *Media Matters in America*, 1 May 2007. http://mediamatters.org.

[25] Andrew Ironside, "Beck said Gore using 'same tactic' in fight against global warming as Hitler did against Jews," *Media Matters in America*, 1 May 2007. http://mediamatters.org.

[26] See the Media Matters file on Glenn Beck. http://mediamatters.org.

[27] John Norris, "Hans Blix Caught Between Iraq and a Hard Place," MTV News, 2007. http://www.MTV.com.

[28] Huffington Post.

[29] Edic Newsroom, quoting COP21 President Laurent Fabius.

[30] Thomas Jefferson, "First Inaugural Address, March 4, 1801," Avalon.

Chapter 9

Plutocracy Rises

"But the most common and durable source of factions has been the various and unequal distribution of property... The regulation of these various and interfering interests forms the principal task of modern legislation and involves the spirit of party and faction in the necessary and ordinary operations of government."
—*James Madison, Federalist Papers, No. 10*[1]

The rise of plutocracy, rule by the wealthy, has been a taboo political subject in America for a long time even though the signs of it have been everywhere and the consequences are fatal to democracy. The two main reasons for this taboo are: a) fear that attacking the rise of plutocracy will cause a backlash that will stop a mythical trickle-down to the masses and b) the grossly mistaken belief that there is an American right to unrestrained wealth accumulation, even though it causes huge social imbalances, great public harm, and criminal abuse of power.

In the quotation above, James Madison declared that the unequal distribution of property was the most common and durable (enduring) source of factions and that regulation and controlling these "interfering interests" was the "principal task" of modern legislation. This is a strong and remarkably foresighted statement by the political centrist who was the father of the Constitution. In 1787 there were many priorities for America and a relatively minor amount of total wealth. Yet Madison foresaw that massive wealth redistribution and plutocracy could be the downfall of America, and that controlling them had to be a principal task.

In the debates on the ratification of the Constitution, Noah Webster, writing under the pseudonym "A Citizen of America," affirmed Madison's view:

"*A general and tolerably equal distribution of landed property is the whole basis of national freedom...* [T]he laborious and saving [persons], who are generally the best citizens, will possess each his share of property and power, and thus the balance of wealth and power will continue where it is, in *the body of the people.*"[2]

Webster echoed Charles Pinckney, who spoke at the Convention, and affirmed the fundamental principle that the balance of wealth and power must be "in the people." Madison was also correct in stating that factions based on money and property are the most persistent of all factions—an invasive vine that smothers democracy. In a separate chapter we examine many of the laws and regulations that have been designed to restrain the growth of plutocracy in America—and have failed.

It was Democratic President Harry Truman, not any follower of Ronald Reagan, who, in 1952 after World War II, appears to have coined the phrase "trickle down" in reference to wealth. Truman said: "Instead of trying to build up the prosperity of the favored few, and letting some of it *trickle down to the rest*, we [Truman's Democratic Party] have been working to raise the incomes of the vast majority of the people."[3]

This statement is plain and sensible and in the public good, like Truman himself. His policies *did* make progress toward the goal of raising the incomes of the vast majority of the people—and not through enrichment of the top 10%.

In 2015, when President Obama raised the issue of rebuilding the middle class and restoring an acceptable balance in America's wealth distribution, Republican Senator Orrin Hatch, the highest legislative representative responsible for managing America's finances enjoying his *seventh* six-year term in the U.S. Senate, howled that Obama was initiating "class warfare."[4] Presumably he was referring to a "class" consisting of 90% of Americans struggling to reclaim representative democracy that existed two or three generations ago. Only a senator who had built himself the kind of personal domain in Congress that the Founders denounced could possess the extraordinary arrogance to characterize this struggle as class warfare. Unfortunately, when Obama examined his odds of success in an infected Congress, he withdrew his proposals. It was a sad and damning commentary on the current state of the union.

I should distinguish at the outset the difference between the evils of plutocracy and the great public good that has sometimes occurred as a result of personal philanthropy. American plutocrats, we shall see, will do literally anything to acquire wealth and will use that wealth for little other than pleasing themselves and acquiring and wielding power and status. The other chapters in the book will introduce the reader to many American plutocrats. Among the rich today, the ratio of plutocrats to philanthropists and patriots has never been higher than in the last three decades. Some of the stories from the days of the American Revolution, the Founding, and the turn of the twentieth century (Theodore Roosevelt's era) are inspiring. At the time of the Revolution Robert Morris and William Bingham were successful entrepreneurs in Philadelphia, close friends, and possibly the richest men in America. (Stephen Girard followed them and made history with his grant of $2 million in 1830's dollars for the construction of Girard College for orphans in Philadelphia.)

General Washington was suffering from large shortages of money and supplies. Morris reached into his pocket and contributed at least $50,000 to the cause.[5] He is known as the "financier of the Revolution." That sort of thing, a spontaneous, large, personal contribution of money to a government leader for the cause of justice and the common good (and without tax deductions for the donor) does not happen any longer even though the U.S. population is more than a hundred times larger. Morris and Bingham both later became U.S. senators at a time when being a senator opened no doors to personal wealth or power. It was *public service*. Even Benjamin Franklin, who had only limited funds to contribute, at one point "collected all his available cash— £4000—and lent it to the Continental government."[6]

General Washington had suffered a string of defeats. Morris developed a daring plan for Bingham to serve the American cause. (Sadly, in later life Morris completely lost his entrepreneurial touch, and was forced into debtors' prison.) The plan was for Bingham to go down to the French West Indies (Martinique) to set up a high-seas privateering venture for the benefit of the war effort. Bingham and his crew would capture British ships and divert the valuable cargo to the Continental Congress for distribution to the Continental Army—or for sale by Congress. Bingham could have remained in Philadelphia comfortably building his financial empire. Nevertheless, he accepted the challenge. His success depended on having courage, skill, money, diplomatic ability in dealing with the French governor in Martinique, and paramount loyalty to America. France was still a neutral country, and many British ships of war and trade sailed through the Caribbean and made port in the islands. Bingham had to be constantly negotiating with French representatives in Martinique to conduct his enterprise. France had not yet agreed to become our ally. Bingham's record was remarkable. By February, 1777, reportedly 250 British vessels with cargo estimated at $10 million had been captured.[7]

Bingham also owned or controlled American vessels trading between the Continent, the West Indies, and Europe that generated additional revenue for America. Nominally, Bingham was a Federalist in Alexander Hamilton's party, but he maintained close friendships with Democratic Republicans in Jefferson's party. According to R.C. Alberts's biography, Bingham courageously broke with his own party on two crucial issues: to save the country from a war with France and to avoid an internal revolution over the choice of a president. There were many instances of him not following the party line. Unfortunately for Bingham, the Continental Congress was not a reliable partner; it occasionally left Bingham unreimbursed even for out-of-pocket expenses. Sometimes Bingham advanced money from his own account when his prizes on the high seas fell short of his projections to Congress.

A similar patriotic spirit guided some of Theodore Roosevelt's friends. The story of the those who founded the National Park Service is well told in a book and film of the same title by Ken Burns and Dayton Duncan: *The National Parks—America's Best Idea.*[8] More than a few powerful politicians in Washington much preferred exploiting the commercial value of the nation's magnificent wild places to preserving them. It was a constant struggle. Roosevelt often ran into a wall of congressmen who refused to acquire lands with federal money *or even to accept them for free when they were donated* because there would be costs of maintenance.

John D. Rockefeller, Jr. famously purchased and held for years the land needed to complete the protection of Yosemite National Park until Congress finally accepted the donation. Stephen Mather was a successful businessman who managed to elevate the status of the Grand Canyon from a National Monument to a National Park. He also became the first director of the National Park Service. Throughout his life he suffered from crushing bouts of mental depression, and one of his worst episodes was ongoing when he met with parties interested in the Grand Canyon crusade. Mather's wife had no choice at that time but to admit him to a sanatorium. Mather frequently retreated to the wilderness for healing, as did Roosevelt, but his disease this time was more devastating. His wife allowed only one art object in his room at the sanatorium—a photograph of Yosemite. For months Mather's assistant managed to run the newly formed National Park Service while its first director was in seclusion. When Mather emerged, he had regained his energy and even his old charm and persistence. He descended on Congress with an irresistible army of proponents, and Grand Canyon National Park was born.

Along the way, Mather personally funded salaries of Park Service employees and met other financial obligations of the Service.

These stories are inspiring, but they are definitely history, not current events.

The first seeds of plutocracy sprouted in the 1890's when the barons of industry built up huge trusts (corporations) and forced the enactment of the federal antitrust laws against monopolies and combinations in restraint of trade. Corporations were forced to divest themselves of parts of the business. For more than the next sixty years, antitrust enforcement was a major sector of law practice and adjudication—for corporate lawyers, the Justice Department's Antitrust Division, the Federal Trade Commission, and federal court judges and court-appointed masters. The tide turned quickly. The reasons for antitrust enforcement certainly did not disappear— on the contrary. The concentration of economic and political power in fewer and fewer mega-corporations and banks demanded *more* antitrust enforcement. What turned the tide was that wealthy individuals and factions were joined by a host of ideologues, so-called Neoconservatives, and *together* they simply overwhelmed the political and governmental process. This was the birth of real plutocracy, identified initially by Roosevelt. Some of the factors that suppressed the rise of plutocracy during the first eighty years of the twentieth century, other than the lack of a dominant Neoconservative faction, were the Depression, Franklin's Roosevelt "New Deal" package of regulatory laws and agencies, and World War II. When the plutocrats finally did gain the upper hand, the biggest changes were alterations of the Internal Revenue Code (discussed later), the gutting of U.S. antitrust enforcement, and the corruption of the Securities and Exchange Commission. Any corporate lawyer contemplating a merger or acquisition will now tell you that European Union antitrust regulators are generally the ones who cause concern to business, not U.S. regulators.

The phrase "too big to fail" was coined by Americans. It is the antithesis of the principles of James Madison and the antitrust statutes. No enterprise should be allowed to reach the stage of threatening to destroy the financial footing of America and millions of public investors. Even following an avalanche of financial and corporate malfeasance that we discuss next, there has been no structural reform that protects the people from a repeat performance—just as there was none after the Savings & Loan collapse in the early 1980's.

The post-WWII economic data show that the American people participated in a return to prosperity on a relatively even and equitable basis. On behalf of the Congressional Budget Office (CBO), Chad Stone performed a data comparison.[9] Initially, the income curves overlapped each other for three categories of the population—the top 5% by income, the median or average percentile, and the bottom 20%. Then in 1979-80, the top 5% broke loose. When thirty years had passed since the post-War era, the bottom 20% of America had made no financial progress, the median population was up approximately 18%, and the top 5% was up 50%. (The median is the preferred means of establishing an average; half of the population is above the number and half below.) The top 1% was "off the chart"—up 314%, after tax, from 1979 to 2007. This picture has been closely examined and updated by two well-known economists with extensive experience in wealth distribution: Emmanuel Saez and Thomas Piketty.[10]

Economists resort to one or more of three databases when conducting these studies. They are maintained by U.S. Census Bureau (the Current Population Survey), the Internal Revenue Service (collected by the Division of Statistics and Income), and the Congressional Budget Office. The differences are described in a recent article by the Center on Budget and Policy Priorities.[11] Briefly, the Census Bureau issues frequent reports but uses a smaller sample of the population (75,000 households), looks at income before taxes, and does not take into account information on persons having incomes exceeding $1 million (it lists them all as persons earning $999,999). These limitations are significant for our purposes. The IRS looks at tax filing units, employs a larger sample (240,000 returns), but does not take into account non-filers or those receiving food and health assistance. The IRS undercounts at the low end and the high end. Using IRS income statistics inherently underestimates the wealth gap for reasons that become clear when we discuss the Internal Revenue Code. Nevertheless, we will use the Saez-Piketty analysis based on IRS data analysis because the statistical analysis is robust and the alternatives are not as good. The Saez-Piketty studies examined individual incomes and shares of total national income and growth captured by the top, median, and lower percentiles of our population.[12] The Pew Research Center, one of the most respected foundations, also has relied on Saez and Piketty.

Parenthetically, the Census Bureau has made some interesting observations regarding retirement-age people. In 2013, the number of people aged 65 and older deemed to be "in poverty" would have *increased by 14.7 million if Social Security payments had been excluded*, thereby quadrupling the number of seniors in poverty.[13] Hopefully, Social Security will hold its own against political attacks, but these figures give us a strong sense that there is no cushion. Furthermore, the U.S. definition of "poverty" is stricter than in other countries.

Moreover, the Employee Benefit Research Institute, as reported by the investment analysis firm Morningstar, points to a $4 trillion "retirement gap."[14] Based on statistics for 44 million people, it appears that slightly more than half of Americans will not have enough money for retirement in the customary manner. In some cases, especially if there are uninsured health costs, the results will be dire.

The Internal Revenue Code was intended to be progressive, i.e., to apply higher tax rates to richer taxpayers and thereby to promote a more even distribution of wealth to meet the Founders' expressed goal. The top-bracket federal income tax rate for individuals rose as high as 91% and remained there from 1954 until 1964. From 1965 to 1982 the top bracket fluctuated between 77% and 70%. Thus, for 28 years—the span of an entire generation—the richest Americans were required to pay from *70% to 90%* of their taxable income to the federal government (not counting state and local taxes). Did business corporations collapse? Were there mass bankruptcies? Did executives flee their posts or commit suicide? Were there mass layoffs of workers and recessions attributable to the impact of these tax rates? Did the middle class wither and die for lack of trickle-down? The answer to all of these questions—the favorite propaganda of the plutocrats—is no. In fact, the progressive-tax-rate era coincided with relative prosperity for the people. There also was no avalanche of corporate malfeasance and financial disaster similar to the succession of events between 1980 and 2010. That was not a coincidence.

The top marginal tax rate declined as Neoconservatives and plutocrats gained more political power in Washington, and politics and the government succumbed more and more to these factions. The top marginal rate plummeted during the George W. Bush administration to approximately 35%, less than half of what it had been. Upper middle-class earners now found themselves being taxed at only a few percentage points less than the superrich; sometimes they fell into the same or even *higher* brackets. Congress was busy creating tax shelters and loopholes for the rich.

Mitt Romney ran for president as a Republican. He was finally compelled to divulge his personal income and taxes. In a functional representative democracy, a presidential candidate's income information would be placed in the public domain as soon as he announces his candidacy. Romney reportedly earned $13.7 million in a single year (2011) and he paid *14.1%* to the government, less than half the nominal tax-bracket rate.[15] In 2010, the previous year, Romney paid federal income taxes at an effective rate of *13.9%.*[16] The Romney story is not an anomaly. Most of the members of the top decile (top 10% by income) and top percentile (top 1%) have many options for enriching themselves and making sure that the cost of government is shifted down to the middle class. This is plutocracy by definition, the most vulgar and offensive form of tyranny, as Theodore Roosevelt said.

In the 1920's, at the peak of the stock market, there was great wealth inequity: the top percentile grabbed almost 24% of total national income. In the Truman years, the outrageous 1-24 ratio fell to a much more equitable 1-9. But by 2007, the top percentile was again taking almost exactly the same percentage as it did in the 1920's—23%.[17] From 1993 to 2010, the top percentile captured *58% of real income growth* in America; the bottom 99% captured *6.4%.* These statistics are appalling.

The impact of recessions tells us more. In the 2007-09 recession, the bottom 99% suffered a significantly larger drop in income than they did in the 2000-02 recession—11.6% down versus 6.5% down. When partial recovery came in 2010, the bottom 99% of income-earning families experienced a real income growth of only 0.2% compared to 11.6% for the top percentile. Thus, ordinary Americans suffered more in the downturns and gained less in the upturns than the rich. This is the cumulative result of all the factors we have discussed—and the disparity in investment opportunities. There has been no structural reform to rectify this inequity.

From the 1950's to the 1970's the top decile took a share of total income of approximately 33%. The top decile ratio has exploded from a 10-33 ratio to 10-48. That means that the top 10% of Americans grabbed 48% of total income. The speed with which this wealth gap opened is attributable to factors beyond income tax policy. Corporate executives, athletes, entertainment figures, and others have become grossly over-compensated. Also, the proliferation of asset-hiding schemes is far out of control. In April 2016, a German newspaper reported that eleven million documents had been released to the International Consortium of Investigative Journalists relating to a Panama law firm's establishment of secret offshore bank accounts and other vehicles to shelter monies for top government leaders, athletes, politicians, and business moguls around the world.[18] Some of the politicians had been publicly claiming to be promoting business transaction transparency. What is new here is that the actors in the secret offshore money handling, money laundering, and tax avoidance included many people holding public office and that the largest havens included places like the British Virgin Islands.

One of the causes of the soaring disparities in wealth between the top decile and the other 90% has been the gross disparity in investment opportunities available to the two groups. For example, the most popular stock (equity) mutual fund for investing in the Standard & Poor's Index ("S&P") of top U.S. companies has been Vanguard's 500 Index Fund Admiral Class. This fund and others like it are found in many employer-employee Section 401(k) retirement accounts. As of March 31, 2016, an investor who had held the line with this fund through the ravages of 2008 would have obtained a 10-year average annual return *before taxes* of 7.0%. When taxes on the distributions made by the fund are taken into account, the return drops to 6.6%. When taxes on the sale of the fund are taken into account, the return drops to 5.65%. Then, of course, there is the cost of inflation. A middle class has endured cost burdens for education, insurance, health care, child care, and so forth that certainly exceed the generic calculation of consumer price inflation. All things considered, the net investment return to the average working American from this well-run, low-cost stock mutual fund has been pitifully small compared to the returns that members of the top decile have captured, whether legally or illegally or both.

Vanguard's top balanced mutual fund containing bonds as well as stocks is Wellington. The respective returns for Wellington over the span of 10 years have been 7.15%, 5.83%, and 5.65%—not significantly different from the S&P Index Fund. The picture darkens considerably as we look into the future.

Wages and salaries have stagnated for a lot of the time during the last ten years. Executive compensation is discussed later. Investment experts like Vanguard founder Jack Bogle and the Morningstar Investment Services now predict that real returns for long-term investors will be *half* of the historic rates.[19] They estimate 4% before taxes.[20]

Meanwhile, in the halls of Wall Street's financial "upstairs," millions of shares are traded in huge blocks on a daily basis, sometimes by computers, sometimes by day traders, and also by hedge funds and other institutions. As a result, there is enormous volatility in the stock indexes. Shares prices go up and down, but the long-term investor, with neither the time nor the money to play with the big boys, makes little progress. The rich take advantage of day trading, speculation, and trading in stock options, futures, commodities, foreign currencies, derivatives, and other exotic securities—as well as private equity firms that take a direct interest in a company or in oil-and-gas, real estate, and other types of partnerships.

An interesting perspective was added in an article that appeared in *The Economist* in June 2016.[21] A new experimental movement is underway, mostly in rich countries, for a "universal basic income" as a partial remedy for the vast, inequitable disparities in wealth and income. The idea is that the simplest and most immediate step would be to enact unconditional cash grants directly to citizens. According to the article, the idea has some roots in the Enlightenment, but that claim seems flimsy. The latest iteration has found support among Silicon Valley plutocrats on the supposed ground that increasing slightly the cash assets of wage-earners would nourish their entrepreneurial instincts. Of course, no one wants a return of the old welfare system that cost a lot and provided strong incentives against leaving the state of joblessness. All in all, while it is interesting that plutocrats are looking at the monstrous wealth and income gap, the universal income proposal seems mostly a way of keeping plutocracy in place and not changing the root causes of it in the first place.

The *Economist* article provided some graphs that support the analysis in this chapter. One table in particular, Gini Coefficients, ranked nations on a scale from "perfect equality" (equal to 0) to "perfect inequality" (equal to 1). Of the thirteen developed countries ranked, the United States ranked farthest *away* from perfect equality and first place for inequality; in fact, between 1985 and the date of the latest tabulation, the U.S. jumped substantially ahead of the country holding second place for inequality. Another table compared the substantial rise in Gross Domestic Product post-2008 to full-time workers' median earnings. *Fourteen years* after 2000 the earnings were still at the same level; they only increased in 2015. Fourteen years of stagnant earnings is a miserable record against any standard, especially considering the inflation in the earlier years, but it is an absolutely terrible record against a substantially rising GDP. The data clearly cannot be dismissed as statistical outliers; they are manifestations of severe malfunction of the American republic.

In the 1970's there were public-interest groups who argued their causes before Congress and the White House, which resulted in substantial improvements in the areas of the environment and public health, consumer safety, public disclosure of government documents, and occupational safety and health. Public-interest groups exist today in these areas and in the area of income inequality, but they have been drawn into fighting the big-moneyed factions on their own terms in the Capital, and they have fared poorly compared to the earlier period when a strong majority of the *American people* came together as citizens with a common interest and demanded major reforms to save the country and the republic. Public interest groups are perennially smothered by armies of former senators, congressmen, and agency officials now lobbying on behalf of factions.[22]

Independent polls conducted by the Pew Research Center have shown that 55% of Republicans surveyed considered the current economic system "fair to most people."[23] Actually, a quick look at the daily voting records of Republicans reveals that this percentage is more like 90% than 55%.

Congress has repeatedly rebuffed calls for a major overhaul of the Internal Revenue Code. In 2012-13 there was only a slight increase in the top marginal income tax rate (from 35% to 39.6%) and the capital gains and dividend tax rates (from 15% to 20%). The threshold for imposing these new rates was set so high (households earning $450,000 and individuals earning $400,000) that millions of Americans who should have been placed in higher tax brackets came away unscathed. The labyrinth of tax shelters, loopholes, and deductions for high-end individuals and corporations remains intact.

One problem is that Americans in general have the false notion that they are overtaxed—a myth promoted by the demagogues to make us believe that "we are all in the same boat." The truth is that among thirty-four countries committed to democracy and market economies (members of the Organisation for Economic Co-operation and Development ["OECD"]) only *two countries* have collected total tax revenues as percentages of Gross Domestic Product *lower* than the U.S.: Mexico and Chile.[24] New York Times columnist Paul Krugman has noted that America is not alone in being the victim of an anti-tax ideological war.[25] France has been vilified by a European Union official and by Standard & Poor's for its approach of using tax increases to reduce deficits and to preserve essential services instead of cutting government spending. European countries differ from the United States in collecting more revenue from taxes on goods and services, e.g., the Value Added Tax, or VAT.

The whole situation was summed up years ago by one of America's most esteemed Supreme Court Justices, Louis D. Brandeis, who lived through the Great Depression. He said: "We can have democracy in this country or we can have great wealth concentrated in the hands of the few, but we can't have both."[26]

Thus, the rise of plutocracy has brought to reality the Founders' worst fears.

---

[1] *Federalist*, Mentor, No. 10, 79.

[2] Noah Webster, "A Citizen of America," 17 October 1787, collected in *The Debate on the Constitution, Part One, Debates in the Press* (New York:

Literary Classics of the United States, Inc., 1993), 129, 157–58 (emphasis in original).

[3] Harry Truman, "Speech at Jefferson–Jackson Day Dinner," 29 March 1952, collected in University of Virginia Miller Center for Public Affairs, Scripps Library, Presidential Speeches.

[4] Reuters, 20 January 2015; http://www.rawstory.com.

[5] Robert C. Alberts, *The Golden Voyage: The Life and Times of William Bingham, 1752–1804* (Boston: Houghton Mifflin, 1969), 47.

[6] Id. at 42.

[7] Id.

[8] Dayton Duncan and Ken Burns, *The National Parks—America's Best Idea* (New York: Knopf, 2009). Film of same name, Ken Burns dir. and Ken Burns and Dayton Duncan, prod., Public Broadcasting Service (2009).

[9] Id.

[10] Emmanuel Saez, "Striking It Richer: The Evolution of Top Incomes in the United States (updated with 2009 and 2010 estimates)"2 March 2012; http://elsa.berkeley.edu/~saez/saez/UStopincomes-2001.pdf. Thomas Piketty and Emmanuel Saez, "Income Inequality in the United States, 1913–2008," *Quarterly Journal of Economics* 118 (1), February 2003, 1–39, updated Piketty and A.B. Atkinson eds. *Oxford University Press* (2007) (Tables and Figures Updated to 2010, March, 2012). Thomas Piketty, *Capital in the Twenty-First Century* (Cambridge: Belknap Press of Harvard University Press, 2014). I have not attempted to compare the journal articles upon which I relied with the 2014 book.

[11] Chad Stone et al., "A Guide to Statistics on Historical Trends in Income Inequality," Center on Budget and Policy Priorities, http://www.ccbpp.org, 17 April 2014.

[12] Emmanuel Saez, "Striking It Richer: The Evolution of Top Incomes in the United States (updated with 2009 and 2010 estimates)" 2 March 2012; http://elsa.berkeley.edu/~saez/saez/UStopincomes-2001.pdf. Thomas Piketty and Emmanuel Saez, "Income Inequality in the United States, 1913–2008," *Quarterly Journal of Economics* 118 (1), February 2003, 1–39, updated Piketty and A.B. Atkinson eds. Oxford University Press (2007) (Tables and Figures Updated to 2010, March, 2012). Thomas Piketty, *Capital in the Twenty-First Century* (Cambridge: Belknap Press of Harvard University Press, 2014). I have not attempted to compare the journal articles upon which I relied with the subsequent book.

[13] Carmen DeDavas-Walt and Bernadette D. Proctor, "Income and Poverty in the United States: 2013," U.S. Census Bureau, Current Population Reports, P60-249 (Washington, DC: U.S. Government Printing Office, 2014).

[14] Scott Cooley, "America's $4 Trillion Retirement Gap," www.Morningstar.com, 27 March 2015.

[15] Jeanne Sahadi, "Romney Paid 14% Effective Tax Rate in 2011," CNN Money, 21 September 2012.

[16] Id.

[17] All of the economic data cited here are drawn from the Saez and Piketty articles listed above. In addition, see Emmanuel Saez, "Striking it Richer: The Evolution of the Top Incomes in the United States (Updated with 2009 and 2010 Estimates)," 2 March 2012, http://elsa.berkeley.edu/~saez/saez/UStopincomes-2010.pdf.

[18] Michael Schmidt and Steven Lee Myers, "Panama Law Firm's Leaked Files Detail Offshore Accounts Tied to World Leaders," *NYT,* 3 April 2016.

[19] Christine Benz, "4 Dangerous Assumptions That Could Hurt Your Retirement," 5 February 2015, Morningstar.com. Jack Bogle/Morningstar, "Bogle: Tough Decade Ahead for Equity Investors," 23 October 2015, Morningstar.com.

[20] Id.

[21] "Sighing for Paradise to Come," 4 June 2016, *The Economist,* 21–24.

[22] Three tax reform groups are: Tax Notes, The Tax Policy Center, and Citizens for Tax Justice.

[23] Drew DeSilver, Pew Research Center, "U.S. Income Inequality, on the rise for decades, is now highest since 1928," Pew Research Center Fact Tank, http://www.pewresearch.org, 5 December 2013.

[24] Organisation for Economic Co-operation and Development, *Table A: Total Tax Revenue as a Percentage of GDP,* http://www.oecd.org/newsroom/41498733.pdf.

[25] Paul Krugman, "The Plot against France," NYT, 10 November 2013, Opinion Pages.

[26] Raymond Lonergan, *Mr. Justice Brandeis, Great American* (1941), 42, collected in Wikiquote, http://www.wikiquote.org.

Chapter 10

Infections in Industry

"[N]othing therefore in my judgment can save us but a total reformation in our own conduct, or some decisive turn to affairs in Europe. The former alas! to our shame be it spoken! is less likely to happen than the latter, as it is now consistent with the views of the Speculators, various tribes of money makers, & stock jobbers of all denominations to continue the War for their own private emolument [gain], without considering that their avarice, and thirst for gain must plunge everything (including themselves) in one Common Ruin."
—*George Washington to George Mason (March 27, 1779)*[1]

General George Washington's 1779 letter to George Mason condemned the avarice and narcissism of the big-money men in terms familiar to us today. At the time, the very existence of a United States of America was much in doubt. Washington perceived only two chances for all Americans to avoid being plunged into "one Common ruin." One was a total reformation in the conduct of the plutocrats, and the other was a major intervention on the side of America by one or more European nations. Fortunately, he received the latter. The first has never happened. Today we have only one choice.

If we have any question regarding whether Congress, post-1980, has reformed itself or the country by enacting the Dodd-Frank Wall Street Reform and Consumer Protection Act (Public Law 111-203— July 21, 2010), we can answer that now. Congress did precisely what everyone expected this political body to do. It bombastically claimed that the new law would "create a sound foundation to grow jobs, protect consumers, rein in Wall Street and big bonuses, end bailouts and 'too big to fail,' [and] prevent another financial crisis."[2] The Act will do none of that. Despite Barney Frank's sincere efforts, the law is perforated with concessions to industry, intentional ambiguities of language, and omissions. Numerous industry lobbyists continue to gnaw away at the law and the executive-branch rulemaking. Dodd-Frank is destined to take its place alongside countless other illusory laws enacted since the original S&L Crisis.

One example is the much-discussed Volcker Rule, a half-hearted attempt to find a substitute for the repealed Glass-Steagall Act that prohibited commercial bankers from taking the risks inherent in investment banking. Commercial banks manage consumer checking and savings accounts, loans and mortgages, personal trusts, and so forth. If the Volcker Rule ever becomes final, it will miss its goal by a wide margin. Paul Volcker himself spoke out sharply in 2014 against the failure of big finance in the wake of the 2008 crisis to make the obvious moves: to reduce the risks unacceptable for those banks upon which the health of the whole U.S. economy depends.[3] There is no place in these banks for exotic securities, excessive leverage (debt), private-equity operations, venture capital, or hedge funds. Volcker said:

> It is striking that the world's leading investment bankers, noted for their cleverness and agility in advising clients on how to restructure companies and even industries, however complicated, apparently can't manage the orderly reorganization of their own activities in more than five years.[4]

In 2015 the *New York Times* reported a "continuing [industry] assault on the 2010 Dodd-Frank law," an assault that has achieved "remarkable success."[5]

> In the span of a month, the nation's biggest banks and investment firms have twice won passage of measures to weaken regulations intended to help lessen the risk of another financial crisis. The firms have set their sights on narrow, arcane provisions and greased their efforts with a surge of lobbying and campaign contributions.[6]

Others have pointed to obvious reasons why effective reform does not happen: the culture of self-dealing on Wall Street and the over-compensation and coddling of top executives who have manifested worse judgment and character than the feudal barons of Theodore Roosevelt's time.[7]

In April 2016, the Federal Reserve System and the Federal Deposit Insurance Corporation (prime regulatory agencies defined below) said that five of eight banks do not have credible plans for winding themselves down in a crisis without creating a mass panic and triggering massive federal bailouts.[8] The lobbying is incessant and overwhelming, as we will see. The federal agencies vacillate. Jamie Dimon continues to rule J.P. Morgan Chase despite record-shattering penalties imposed on his bank for breaches of federal law. He is unique in holding the positions of *both* Chief Executive Officer and Chairman of the Board that supposedly oversees all the executives. When challenged about the refusal to clean house in the wake of all the violations and give some meaning to Dodd-Frank, he just pointed in other directions.

A Corporation's Right to Exist

A corporation is a legal fiction. It is not a natural person, and it has no right to come into existence except in accordance with the Business Corporation Laws of the various states ("BCL's"). A BCL is entirely distinct from the federal laws and regulations; the BCL standards apply to all business corporations incorporated in the United States. They are the cornerstone for the construction of corporate America. The reasoning behind these laws and the standards they impose are easy to grasp.

Corporations came into existence because: a) entrepreneurs sought huge amounts of money (capital) to build their businesses; b) this money had to come from members of the public on the outside (individually and through pension and retirement funds, unions, trusts, and the like); c) those investors needed access to financial and business information that was truthful and complete as well as assurance that the management handling their money would abide by reasonable standards; and d) the entrepreneurs would not go forward with public corporations unless they could limit their personal liability and avoid being wiped out when businesses went sour. These factors were all placed on the table for evaluation by the states. The state legislatures adopted the legal system of checks and balances embodied in the BCL's. Two bedrock rules govern business corporations and their managements: the Prudent Business Judgment Rule ("BJR") and the Fiduciary Responsibility Rule ("FRR").

The BJR requires managers to exercise prudent business judgment in the best interest of the corporation based on all relevant information reasonably available at the time. "Prudent" means wise, good, and sound in a business sense in the eyes of an ordinary man on the street. "Reasonably available" means available through reasonable inquiry; it is not a defense for an executive to say that he was unaware of critical information if it was in existence, relevant, and accessible to him. When management and a corporate board contemplate an action, e.g., investing heavily in exotic securities, they are legally bound to consider all the risk factors and to exercise prudent business judgment in the best interest of the company and the investors.

The FRR establishes a *duty of trust* owed by management to investors and to the company to handle investments in good faith, honestly, in the best interest of investors and the company, and without any intent to defraud or to conduct self-dealing. This duty goes beyond the ban against basic financial crimes like fraud, conspiracy, theft, and embezzlement. Corporate management has a higher duty. An executive is not allowed to gamble with company money as if it were his own. A fiduciary duty is a duty of faith held by the corporate executive *to the public investors*; the investors place their trust in the fiduciary. The interests of the investors are paramount.

The FRR is intertwined with the BJR. If the standards are violated by management, there should be heavy legal consequences because the public harm can be—and has been—devastating. The avalanche of malfeasance profiled in this chapter raises a number of questions. Why should corporations that repeatedly violate the BCL rules, knowingly and willfully, not suffer the ultimate penalty—having their corporate charters revoked? Making a company pay a money fine to the government rarely produces the major changes that are required from recalcitrant managements.

Also, there must be individual accountability. It is a simple proposition of human behavior known for millennia. Executives responsible for monstrous fraud and the loss of billions of dollars of public investments must be prosecuted individually, fined, incarcerated, and removed from positions of corporate authority. This has not happened in more than 90% of the cases. Our criminal justice system has prosecuted minor street crime more aggressively.

A fundamental flaw is that the states themselves have become corrupted and are more focused on attracting big businesses than maintaining the rule of law. They are joined by corporate lawyers who argue for the most lenient standards and court interpretations of the standards. It is an area that calls out for uniform standards of prudent business judgment and fiduciary duty to be enacted based on legal formulations by the American Law Institute and American Bar Association. In the case synopses below, it is astonishing how federal judges and trustees were "unable to find" sufficient evidence of violations of these two rules. A person with no legal training but with common sense and integrity would not have had this difficulty.

In addition to the two fundamental rules of management conduct, there is a host of federal laws, regulations, and standards, many of which are traceable back to America's remedial response to the Great Depression.

Federal Regulation of Business Corporations to Protect the Public

Chronologically, the first federal regulatory agency established to regulate corporations was the Federal Reserve System (the "Fed"). The Fed is the outgrowth of the First and Second Banks of the United States. The Fed is composed of board members from each region of the country who are experts in finance. The Fed controls the nation's money supply, the interest rates, and the availability of credit. It manages the nation's monetary system, and it regulates banking. When the real estate and sub-prime mortgage binge occurred during the two terms of the George W. Bush administration (the seeds were sown before), the Fed Chair had duties with respect to annual reporting by mortgage lenders under the Home Mortgage Disclosure Act.

The Chairman of the Fed has long acted as a potentate accepted by business, government, and the people to steer the American economy. Before 2008, while Wall Street banks, corporations, and the rating agencies (Standard & Poor's and Moody's) were rotting with corruption, the Fed was mumbling at its meetings about inflation (not even on the horizon) and generally looking the other way. The present Fed Chair is a woman whose record is short. She seems level-headed and sincere. Over the years, however, the Chair has told Congress what it, the United States president, and Wall Street, wanted to hear. As we discuss elsewhere, this pandering to factions and the public remains one of the most devastating root causes of the systemic disease, America's civic breakdown.

The financial safety net also includes executive-branch departments like the Department of the Treasury and so-called independent regulatory agencies like the Securities and Exchange Commission (SEC), the Federal Trade Commission (FTC) (charged with enforcing the antitrust laws along with the Antitrust Division of the Justice Department), and the Federal Deposit Insurance Corporation (FDIC). To these bodies we must add a formidable array of Congressional oversight committees supported by their own Government Accounting Office and the Congressional Budget Office. This armada, *assuming it was not corrupted*, should have been quite adequate to protect the nation against the avalanche of financial and corporate crime summarized below.

The Avalanche of Malfeasance

The Savings & Loan Crisis of the 1980's was actually the first outbreak of the systemic disease. Various portrayals of this crisis can be found online.[9] Savings and Loans or S&L's (also, called "thrifts") were regulated by the Federal Home Loan Bank Board and other agencies. According to one source, 1,043 of 3,234 S&L's collapsed. A combined asset base of more than $300 billion was lost in the collapse and had to be reconstituted in whole or in part with federal funds by a special bailout and reconstruction agency, the Resolution Trust Company. It was a financial disaster brought on by greed, self-dealing, and a blatant industry-wide breach of the business-law rules of fiduciary duty and prudent business judgment. Despite the enormity of this implosion, S&L managers escaped individual liability and criminal sentences. This failure to impose *individual liability* on businessmen who callously disregarded standards of conduct established to protect the public represented a breakdown in the system of checks and balances that state legislatures had modeled on Madison's principles. The S&L Crisis set a disastrous precedent for the future.

S&L managers had become unsatisfied with their roles as consumer bankers, and they wanted to take on the risks of investment banking in the hope of securing larger rewards. In the post-Depression years, Congress had erected a supposed wall (the Glass-Steagall Act) between commercial banking and investment banking. Commercial bankers lusted for the potential rewards of investment banking. Of course, the risks were much higher. Congress did not just amend Glass-Steagall to open some doors for the bankers; it repealed the law entirely.

The back story of the S&L's is that they had persuaded the Federal Home Loan Bank Board to lower the standards for capital reserves to be held by the banks. Having lower reserves equates to allowing higher leverage or borrowing and, of course, more risk. The S&L's also inflated the values of the assets on their books to permit more borrowing—which misled third parties. Another cause was misjudgment of the volatile interest rate swings of the time.

One of the most infamous cases of S&L corruption was the "Keating Five"—named for the five influential *senators* whom the politically well-connected Charles Keating of the Lincoln S&L persuaded to pressure the Bank Board and other agencies for relaxed regulation of S&L's. The collapse of the Lincoln S&L was one of the largest of all S&L failures. It was a textbook case of greed and corruption.

When S&L failures multiplied, it became such a bad situation that the Federal Savings & Loan Insurance Corporation (FSLIC) that insured S&L's became insolvent (unable to pay its debts) and merged into the Federal Deposit Insurance Corporation (FDIC). The Office of Thrift Supervision (OTS), an arm of the Treasury Department, assumed regulatory responsibility jointly with the FDIC for the regulation of thrifts. But it was not long after the S&L Crisis that the safety net was tested again. The case involved Washington Mutual (WaMu), the nation's largest thrift. The federal agencies had good forewarning of the WaMu collapse. Indy Mac was a similar large thrift in the American west. Indy Mac failed in July, 2008, which should have put all of the regulators on high alert. WaMu collapsed spectacularly in September, 2008—the largest bank failure in U.S. history. WaMu was also the largest institution regulated by the Office of Thrift Supervision.[10]

WaMu had $300 billion in assets. It would have been logical to assume that, because of the 1980's S&L Crisis, WaMu would have been placed at the top of a watch list by federal agencies. But for seven years, from 2001 through 2007, as WaMu assumed more and more risk in the mortgage loan and derivatives market, the OTS continued to assign WaMu a risk rating of 2, one notch below the best rating of 1. WaMu leveraged its huge growth by enticing the *least* creditworthy borrowers to obtain mortgage loans and credit cards. The public was duped by quasi-public financial rating agencies, like Standard & Poor's ("S&P"), into believing that all was well at WaMu.

The FDIC disagreed with OTS and concluded that WAMU needed $5 billion in capital to withstand future losses. OTS held its position against the FDIC. WaMu collapsed in September. Just like that, the 118-year-old S&L ceased to exist. Shareholders and bondholders were expected to be wiped out; employees lost jobs. It was a stunning blow to public confidence. (The CEO reportedly retained his $11.6 million cash severance and $7.5 million signing bonus.)[11] The WaMu collapse was the subject of an Inspector General report. The IG found that the FDIC could have stepped in to act as the primary regulator of WaMu, but had instead decided it was "easier to use moral suasion to attempt to convince the O.T.S. to change its rating." That a federal regulatory agency would be more worried about ruffling the feathers of another agency than protecting the public against the largest bank collapse in U.S. history is a shocking thought, really.

Several years before WaMu's collapse, in 1998, a huge hedge fund, Long-Term Capital Management (LTCM), had imploded. A hedge fund is a pooled investment vehicle, privately organized and focused on serving wealthy individuals and institutions. At that time, some three thousand hedge funds handled between $200 and $300 billion in invested capital. These funds typically took much greater risks than, for example, mutual funds. The hedge funds leveraged the $300 billion in capital to $1 trillion through a series of maneuvers involving raising debt, selling short (gambling that a security will fall in value), speculating on foreign currency values, and issuing and trading mortgage-backed and other forms of exotic securities. LTCM had a leverage ratio of approximately 25-1. LTCM held $126 billion in positions and only $4.8 billion in actual capital. LTCM exhibited the same pattern of greed and excess leverage that had brought down the S&L's. When the fund, operating under the secrecies permitted hedge funds because they were not regulated by the SEC, reported more than 40% returns in 1995 and 1996, banks and pension funds flooded in with their money. LTCM went from an infant venture to a purported $1 trillion enterprise. When it collapsed, it sparked a panic on Wall Street.

The key facts and lessons for our purposes are contained in a 43-page joint-agency task force report entitled "Hedge Funds, Leverage, and the Lessons of Long-Term Capital Management: Report of the President's Working Group on Financial Markets (April 1999)." The president was Bill Clinton.

It is worth noting that the Fed considered the bankruptcy of LTCM, or at least some of the Fed officials including the Chairman considered the bankruptcy that would have forced out management and a reorganization and brought in the court, unacceptable. This happened under Clinton, again a very unhealthy precedent. The Fed Chair brokered a deal with fifteen banks putting in $3.5 billion and the Fed taking monetary action to calm the market.

The LTCM Report, by its own title, contained *lessons* to guide Wall Street away from further financial breakdowns. The top financial agencies in the country made urgent recommendations for reform: the Department of the Treasury, the Federal Reserve, the FDIC, the Comptroller of Currency, the Council of Economic Advisers, the Office of Thrift Supervision, the National Economic Council, and the SEC. The Congressional banking committees and the industry undoubtedly scrutinized this report.

In a healthy democratic republic this Report would have resulted in top-priority remedial action by industry, Congress, and the executive branch. Instead, the presidentially commissioned report was buried by the Bush administration and allies on the Hill. That act would have qualified as a major criminal conspiracy if it had been perpetrated in the private sector; however, in the public sector, the principle of governmental immunity reigns. The LTCM Report bluntly stated that the mainstream financial institutions upon which the entire American economy depends were much too highly leveraged (not just hedge funds), and they were intertwined with each other as counterparties, thereby inviting a domino-type collapse across the whole financial sector. For example, Merrill Lynch and Bear Stearns handled the trading of the risky securities that LTCM bought and sold, *and* ML and BS *also invested in LTCM*. The report found that the five largest investment banks had a huge impact on the financial stability of America; they had a leverage ratio of 27-1. The Report noted that even commercial banks that held deposit accounts and were traditionally the most solid and conservative members of the banking community had a leverage ratio of 17-1. Securities firms were listed in the same range.

The Report urgently recommended that the following reforms be instituted: a) risk management systems be overhauled and improved by the regulators, b) the adequacy of capital reserves be evaluated, c) bank disclosure and reporting obligations be strengthened, d) the SEC obtain and make available information relating to intertwined counterparties, and e) derivatives dealers be directly regulated.

Shortly thereafter, the giant energy company Enron collapsed in a sea of fraud and corruption, and the Bush administration proceeded hastily in a direction *opposite* to that recommended in the Report. Bush eviscerated many types of business regulation and appointed "regulators" who became pawns of industry. There are many examples—from the SEC to the Interior Department's Mining and Minerals Management Service responsible for regulating oil drilling in the Gulf of Mexico.

The SEC had been created in 1934 in response to the Great Depression for the purpose of regulating financial securities. It is one of the so-called independent regulatory agencies not within the president's cabinet and supposedly not as subject to political influence. Nevertheless, the president is allowed to appoint members to the SEC for five-year terms, with not more than three of five members coming from one political party. A rotation rule prevents the president from appointing all the members at the start of his administration, but within only two years most presidents typically have appointed a majority. Under the Bush administration the SEC rapidly became a servant of industry.

The banks on Wall Street wanted to avoid regulation by the European Union for their operations located there—and particularly any EU regulation of the new wave of exotic securities, including mortgage derivatives. The banks even wanted to reduce the capital reserve requirements that protected investors. In April 2004, five SEC members reportedly met in a basement room to consider the EU requests. They gutted the net capital rule. They decided to tell the EU that they were setting up a new division to regulate bank holding companies dealing in exotic securities. In truth, the Commission reportedly assigned *seven* people to review the operations of holding companies with combined assets of $4 trillion. By September 2008, not a single review had been performed.[12]

The SEC Chairman later made the superfluous admission that "voluntary regulation" does not work. We had learned that lesson a century before.

The SEC led the Committee of European Securities Regulators to believe that the two bodies would be working together, conducting regular good-faith discussions of related issues, specifically the regulation of hedge funds and the credit rating companies like Standard & Poor's.[13] With these assurances, the EU stepped back. This was another fraud.

The credit rating companies actually played a significant role in the financial and corporate collapse. These quasi-governmental entities exist only to assess the creditworthiness of municipal governments, banks, private corporations, and the securities they issue. The investing public relies upon S&P's supposedly independent ratings, but S&P was paid handsomely by the investment banks that issued the exotic securities. S&P therefore issued favorable ratings. S&P was later prosecuted and entered into a settlement whereby S&P paid $1.375 billion in penalties, but again no executives or other managers were prosecuted and the company did not admit guilt.[14] These types of settlements simply do not change bad behavior that has become endemic in large corporations. As Alexander Hamilton had commented, individuals in a group or faction hide behind—and are emboldened by—their group identity.

The following are brief synopses of other cases:

1. "Wages Even Wall Street Can't Stomach"[15]

The Michael Milken case was really the first one to signal a tectonic shift in the culture and attitude on Wall Street. Milken became chief of the high-yield bond department at a famous investment bank, Drexel. According to reports, he took home *$1 billion during a four-year* *period.* It was a staggering display of greed and lawlessness. Drexel collapsed. Milken was indicted on ninety-eight counts of securities fraud, insider trading, and racketeering. In 1990, he entered into a plea bargain to testify against former colleagues in return for a reduction in the charges. His guilty plea earned him a ten-year prison sentence (later reduced) and a permanent ban from the securities industry. Milken was forced to pay $400 million to injured investors as part of a larger package.

2. "AIG to Pay $800 Million to Settle Securities Fraud Charges"[16]

According to Forbes (2008), the American International Group (AIG), originally an insurance company, became the eighteenth largest company in the world. The formerly well-respected AIG plunged into the business of handling exotic securities. It has been estimated that AIG perched atop a trillion-dollar mountain of security assets; credit default swaps—essentially insurance contracts given to banks for pools of mortgages and loans—constituted $440 billion. The company had bet more than *twice* the whole value of the company. The rating agencies held onto an AA rating for AIG. Executives committed accounting fraud and bid-rigging, traded heavily in collateralized debt obligations and credit default swaps, and precipitated a liquidity crisis at AIG.[17] Sub-prime loans were buried in the base of the investment tier. The Fed and other top economic officials apparently believed that if AIG failed, it would produce a domino effect that might plunge the country into a second Great Depression. Whether that was true is highly debatable. The Fed undertook a $160 billion bailout of AIG in 2008. Two executives pleaded guilty to criminal fraud.[18]

3. "Court-Appointed Lehman Examiner Unveils Report"[19]

Lehman Brothers Holdings Inc. was a huge investment bank with 150 years of history. Lehman, like AIG, threw billions of dollars into exotic securities—and steadfastly maintained that all was well at the company. On January 29, 2008, Lehman reported record earnings of $4 billion on revenues of $60 billion. The stock soared to $65 per share. As a court examiner later reported, Lehman began to hide debt from its balance sheet. As rumors spread, Lehman did exactly what the corporation law states should *not* be done in such circumstances. It deluded the public into believing that there was no liquidity crisis at the company. In June 2008, the company reported that it had boosted liquidity to $45 billion. On September 10, 2008, the company issued a press release stating that it had a liquidity pool of $42 billion—a statement difficult to reconcile with the fact that five days later it declared bankruptcy. It was the largest bankruptcy in U.S. history. It set in motion a cascade of financial institution failures.

Ernst & Young was Lehman's certified public accountant. In April 2015, a New York Times writer described how 2008 was sputtering to an end with many corporate settlements, many refusals to admit liability, and almost no prosecutions of responsible individuals—a record that in past years would have subjected the Justice Department and the White House to intense criticism.[20] Ernst paid $10 million for accounting fraud and said they were "pleased to put this matter behind them with no findings of wrongdoing."

Furthermore, before the collapse, officials from the SEC and the Fed had been keeping offices *inside* Lehman's headquarters supposedly to oversee daily the sound management and accuracy of reporting. The onsite review began in March 2008. The SEC reportedly had a practice of deferring to the Fed regarding the larger issues of bank regulation. Lehman failed the stress tests specifically designed by the Fed, but still the Fed did not blow the whistle. The appearance of collusion between the Fed, SEC officials, and Lehman was not overlooked by outside observers.[21] In the end, the court-appointed examiner, in a nine-volume report, said he could not find even a breach of the Business Judgment Rule or the fiduciary duty to shareholders, an astounding result.[22] If, on these facts, there was no breach, it is hard to imagine any circumstances in which the rules could be deemed to have been violated.

4. "Former S.E.C. Lawyer Pleads Guilty in Dreier Case"[23]

In one of the most publicized cases, a *former SEC enforcement lawyer* pleaded guilty to conspiring in the Dreier case to commit securities fraud that involved cheating hedge funds out of millions of dollars. Hedge funds have proved to be magnets for financial wrongdoing.

5. "Hedge Fund Fraud: $291.8 Million Guilty Plea"[24]

There are so many hedge fund fraud cases that it is impossible to summarize them here. One Internet blog is devoted to the subject,[25] as is another with respect to mortgage fraud.[26] It was reported by the Hedge Fund Lounge that a Chicago manager of a hedge fund, Lake

Shore Asset Management, pleaded guilty to a fraud scheme that continued throughout the years 2002–07 and that victimized approximately 900 investors by taking money fraudulently for trading in futures.

6. "S.E.C. Fines Didn't Avert Stanford Group Case"[27]

The SEC imposed a series of relatively small fines on the Stanford Group for securities violations—incidents that should have been red flags for the Commission. Instead the Commission stood aside as Robert Allen Stanford put together an alleged $8 billion fraud. Reportedly, Stanford contributed $2.4 million to a number of federal political candidates. He was a friend and supporter of various congressmen, and these relationships, coupled with the SEC's inertia, enabled Stanford to extend his grasp to the extent of a staggering $8 billion.

7. "S.E.C. Says It Missed Signals on Madoff Fraud Case"[28]

Bernard Madoff, with the help of his accountant, defrauded investors of allegedly $40 billion, the largest financial fraud in the history of the United States conducted by less than a handful of persons. The fraud extended to persons in 119 countries and spawned, as of this writing, claims of $40 billion to a Justice Department victim-relief fund. Along the way, a financial analyst had contacted the SEC directly—more than once—and told them bluntly that Madoff's claimed investment performance was impossible during the years in question and therefore had to be fraudulent. The SEC rejected the analyst's complaints during 2000–2001, and again during 2005–2007. The Madoff Ponzi scheme case is a rarity in that individuals actually went to jail.[29] Madoff pleaded guilty to defrauding investors of billions of dollars; the female controller pleaded guilty to conspiracy, falsifying books and records, and false filings with the SEC. On May 19, 2015, the judge sentenced her to time served because of her prompt and assiduous cooperation with the government—and her expression of "genuine" remorse. She forfeited property.

8. "Tyco to Pay $3 Billion to Settle Investor Lawsuits"[30]

In this case, the company's in-house lawyer allegedly "borrowed" $14 million from the company and did not disclose the transaction. The two top executives stole millions and went to jail. Even a *director* pleaded guilty to fraud. The company settled with class action investors for $3 billion.

9. "WorldCom Investors to Get $6.1 Billion"[31]

Telecommunications giant WorldCom, that had once reached an asset value of $180 billion, collapsed into bankruptcy after its management perpetrated a massive accounting fraud. In this case, the two banks that underwrote and traded the securities, Citigroup and J.P. Morgan Chase, were forced to pay $2.58 billion and $2 billion, respectively, in a suit by investors. The CEO was convicted of fraud.

10. "Regions Financial—Lawsuit Is Settled for $90 Million"[32]

The financial fraud avalanche included both regional players as well as the big Wall Street banks. Regions Financial Corp. was charged with fraud in their financial statements between February 2008 and January 2009. Regions had already agreed to pay $51 million to settle state and federal lawsuits for failure to disclose bad loans.

11. "U.S. is Seeking Felony Pleas by Big Banks"[33]

As the post-2008 prosecutions began to wind down, it became obvious that despite the colossal scale of brazen white-collar crime, the Justice Department had failed to prosecute *corporate individuals* in many of the worst cases. If these criminals did not deserve jail terms, who did, and why would an Attorney General think that collecting some fines from a billion-dollar company would produce the massive changes needed in individual conduct, corporate culture, and corporate structure? Considering what had happened and the extent of publicity, it was shocking to read of an *upsurge* in a two forms of corporate crime: insider stock trading and bank manipulation of the prices of foreign currencies traded. A February 2015 New York Times article stated that the U.S. Attorney General might be seeking felony pleas of guilty by some of the big banks instead of the usual settlements in which the defendant admits nothing and pays money, thereby avoiding bad press, major pressure from customers, and guilty-plea fact-findings that could be used in court by injured parties.[34] The currency trading schemes involve computer programs freezing the execution of a currency trade until it is determined that the volatile currency will not decrease in value and provide the bank with a last-minute chance to pocket profits on the deal. As of the date of writing there has been no new wave of felony prosecutions of individuals or of guilty pleas, in other words, no strengthening of Justice Department enforcement. Deutsche Bank paid an $800 million fine, the largest fine in the history of the Commodity Futures Trading Commission—again, just money.[35]

12. "J.P. Morgan Faulted on Controls and Disclosure in Trading Loss"[36]

J.P. Morgan Chase, the nation's largest bank, was once referred to as America's flagship bank. It is now infamous for dozens of post-2008 lawsuits for fraudulent, deceptive, and manipulative banking practices.[37] JPM entered into a $13 billion settlement with the Department of Justice, mainly related to mortgage-backed securities. The penalty set a record, but it obviously did not reform the bank or punish or oust responsible executives and traders. Fines and penalties have reached approximately $20 billion. JPM management later confessed to repeating the same conduct that triggered the claims in a post-2008 episode of "flawed, complex and poorly reviewed" trading in credit default swaps, resulting in a $6 billion loss. In 2013, a 300-page Congressional Report concluded that JPM's management had misled the comptroller, understated losses, ignored risks and internal controls, manipulated documents, and refused to cooperate in good faith with Congressional investigators.

After the Dodd-Frank law went into effect and JPM shareholders were given the right to cast a non-binding vote against exorbitant, unearned executive pay, a neutral advisory firm, Institutional Shareholder Services (ISS), did recommend a no vote on the compensation for the JPM CEO and Chairman, James Dimon. Nevertheless, 78% (and the following year 61%) of the voters *approved* the payment of $20 million to Dimon. The negative comments in the news and the billions of dollars of fines did not alter the culture at the nation's former flagship bank. Moreover, Dimon held the positions of Chief Executive Officer *and* Board Chairman overseeing the CEO, a blatant conflict of interest that makes a mockery of the whole corporate system. In two elections, only 32% and 36% of those voting followed the ISS recommendation to divide the positions.[38]

13. "Morgan Stanley Reaches $1.25 Billion Mortgage Settlement"[39]

Morgan Stanley was also one of the venerable investment houses on Wall Street. Like the other big banks, it binged on the sale of mortgage-loan derivative securities and misrepresented the underlying risk. The default rates on these bundled-loan securities reached as high as 70%. Morgan Stanley had to pay $1.25 billion to the Federal Housing Finance Agency to resolve claims. The FHFA sued eighteen similar financial institutions. Deutsche Bank's settlement was for $1.92 billion.

14. Insider-Trading Cases

Illegal insider trading *escalated* after 2008 even while many eyes were fastened on Wall Street corruption. On December 7, 2011, the U.S. Attorney in Manhattan was reported to have prosecuted fifty-six individuals for insider trading since taking office in August, 2009, *fifty-three of whom had pleaded guilty or been convicted.* The escalation was proof that the large corporate fines and consent decrees and the bad publicity neither punished nor deterred this gang of wrongdoers and certainly did not alter or reform the financial industry.

It is important to understand two things. First, a lot of taxpayer money is required to launch and carry forward a single federal prosecution. In the United States the winning litigant does not recover attorneys' fees except in limited circumstances. Therefore, the taxpayers have paid millions of dollars that will never be recovered to prosecute financial and corporate criminals. Second, only a fraction of crime is prosecuted. Believe it or not, while there is great waste in the federal government for various reasons, the resources for bringing to justice violators of federal statutes—and for adjudicating the cases—are limited. Therefore, it is good prosecutorial judgment to make the most of every case—to take to court a sampling of the most outrageous and visible wrongdoers, to press for verdicts or guilty pleas, and to force structural change so that there will not be endless repetition of the malfeasance and harm to innocent people. Sadly, this has not occurred.

In one notable insider case, a billionaire executive of the Galleon Group (a hedge fund) conspired with a member of Goldman Sachs, the most prestigious of all investment houses. The Goldman individual reportedly gave advance notice to the Galleon executive of a negative company earnings report so that he could reap millions of dollars by trading before the public knew. U.S. District Judge Richard J. Holwell sentenced the executive to eleven years in jail and declared that there was "a virus in our business culture that needs to be eradicated."[40]

Judge Holwell stands out as someone who perceived gross injustice, appropriately punished it, and tried to establish a meaningful deterrent.

An insider-trading case involving SAC Capital Advisors followed a bizarre course. Initially, six former employees and the firm itself pled guilty. A jury convicted a senior employee, and the firm paid a record fine for a hedge fund, $1.2 billion.[41] The U.S. Attorney commented after the prosecution that insider trading at the firm had been "substantial, pervasive, and on a scale without precedent in the history of hedge funds."[42] SAC did business with the top players on Wall Street: J.P. Morgan Chase and Goldman Sachs. Then, an appellate court reversal led the U.S. Attorney to drop charges against seven individuals.[43] The conclusion of the criminal case then allowed an administrative law judge to lift the stay of proceedings in a civil case by the SEC against Steven A. Cohen, the billionaire owner. There was only *one* count pending. The message sent was that the billionaire owner of a hedge fund can hand off the trades to employees, avoid criminal prosecution for massive insider trading, and expect only a one-count civil case.

15. "How MF Global's 'missing' $7.5 billion was lost and found"[44]

The story of Jon Corzine and MF Global ("MFG") is notable because Corzine was a former U.S. senator, Governor of New Jersey, and CEO of Goldman Sachs—in other words a man who had climbed to the top of both the political and business ladders. He then became CEO of his own financial company, MF Global, a commodities broker. The Commodities Futures Trading Commission ("CFTC") regulates this industry.

MF Global collapsed into bankruptcy in October 2011. Reportedly, Corzine had needed to cover an overdraft at J.P. Morgan.[45] He told his assistant treasurer to "fix it." The evidence showed that there was no other recourse but for her to move $200 million from a segregated customer account—a gross violation of CFTC rules—and that Corzine surely knew it. Corzine did not notify CFTC—another violation. The company plunged into bankruptcy anyway, and the CFTC filed an action in federal court. The CFTC settled with the company and the corporate affiliate for restitution of certain monies to clients, and the litigation proceeded against Corzine and the assistant treasurer.

Nearly $1 billion of client funds went out the door at MFG. A Manhattan lawyer was appointed to seize whatever MFG assets he could find, most of which turned out to be in the U.K. and Canada.[46] The clients were deprived of their money for two years (without interest). The breach of fiduciary duty is obvious. Corzine went on to other financial business.

Executive Compensation Has Been Inversely Correlated with Good Performance

A root cause of disease in industry is the incestuous relationship between boards of directors and the executives they are supposed to oversee. Many directors are themselves chief executive officers and therefore in conflict-of-interest mode. The proof, of course, is in the avalanche of malfeasance and the levels of executive compensation. For decades there have been attempts to create "shareholder democracy" whereby the shareholders and bondholders would have more input on major decisions and compensation. The most recent was the "say-on-pay" rule of the Dodd-Frank legislation. Once again, the industry lobby managed to make the final provision a non-binding vote on compensation, and recent experience shows that very few grossly overpaid executives, even those with mediocre to atrocious records of delivering good profits legally, have been moved out of office or had compensation cut. Here are the facts regarding executive compensation.

Sixty percent of executive compensation is in the form of stock, not salary. Stock options and payments were invented years ago to reward managers for outstanding performance that is easily measured by various ratios using stock price, sales, earnings, book value, and so forth. The incentive system has collapsed. Executives now obtain the stock even in poor years. The disparity between management performance on the one hand and the levels of executive compensation on the other has been shocking. *Forbes* (the business journal) and the AFL-CIO (the labor-union federation) both track executive compensation paid in stock and money from year to year. In 2011, Forbes found that not only had executives not paid a price for their wrongdoing, they had gained increased compensation for performance that was decidedly inferior. The CEO's of the 500 largest companies in America took a 16% increase in compensation for that year, while the average worker received a 3% increase, barely enough to offset inflation.

According to the AFL-CIO, the average worker salary was $34,000 in the same year—and $36,134 in 2014.[47] Thus, the ratio of CEO compensation to average-worker pay has soared from 42–1 to 380–1. In 2011, the top 100 CEO's were compensated in amounts ranging from $18 million to $378 million *per year*. The AFL-CIO Executive Paywatch has calculated an *average* CEO compensation of $12.9 million.

Assume for the purpose of argument that a middle class American earns $130,000 in a year. Under this hypothetical, a CEO earns in a single year one hundred times the amount of a middle class earner's salary and more than twice the amount the individual would earn over an entire 40-year career. With very few exceptions, CEO's are not geniuses who singlehandedly revolutionize a company or an industry. These compensation levels cannot be justified.

A persuasive article on this subject was written by Edward E. Lawler for *Forbes*.[48] Lawler pulverized the justifications put forth by executives and directors for the stratospheric compensation packages. Executives do not abandon top posts if their pay packages drop down into the earth's atmosphere. Moreover, overcompensation "significantly affects the profitability of even relatively large corporations," and it encourages executives to take risky and illegal actions. "There is an enormous societal gap between the top earners in the country and the rest of the country."[49]

Remedies

Many remedies for the private sector are obvious from the manifestations of disease we have discussed. Any regimen that addresses government but not industry or vice versa is bound to fail, as Theodore Roosevelt and others said. Some elements of a good regimen are the following.

The Long-Term Capital Management Report recommendations were clear and unambiguous in 1999, and they must be implemented.

There is no excuse, other than corruption, for not following through on them. The Dodd-Frank law is a flawed response.

Opening up the corporations to the shareholders and employees is essential, and the German model should be studied. Germany adopted a two-tier corporate board system. A Supervisory Board ("SB") may have twenty members. The best thinking is that the number should be limited to twelve.[50] Depending on the number of company employees, up to half of the SB may be elected by the *employees* and the remainder by the *shareholders*. The chairman, who has the deciding vote in the case of deadlocks, must be a shareholder representative. The SB appoints the Management Board ("MB"), decides the executive compensation, is included by the MB in the consideration of all actions involving any fundamental impact on assets and finances of the business before a final decision is made, and must give prior consent to the final decision. It is an explicit duty of the MB to advise the SB "without delay and comprehensively" with regard to business developments and planning, and matters of significance with regard to risk management and compliance. The MB cannot implement business decisions requiring board approval without the SB's own approval.

This German system employs three levels of risk management in: the MB (which must have its own risk management system), the SB, and the auditors (assigned by the SB). The auditors report directly to the SB in order to prevent management from tampering with the audit report, i.e., cooking the books. At the annual meeting, the SB must declare whether the corporation has complied with, and will comply with, the recommendations of the German Corporate Governance Code.

Germany has been making an effort to promote transparency and ethical behavior in business. Members of the boards have a duty to comply with standards and to *report noncompliance by others*. There must be an "adequate number" of independent members on the SB. There is also an emphasis on education and training of corporate officials. German corporations have codes of ethics that seem clear and enforceable. Hopefully, the immense Volkswagen vehicle-emission scandal is a statistical outlier.

An obvious reform now proposed by the first of *six* federal agencies regulating financial firms is to defer for four years half of the bonuses paid to top employees, "significant risk takers," and persons judged to be exposing the firm to "material financial loss."[51] While there are reportedly a dozen banks in the U.S. having more than $250 billion in total assets not including client assets and therefore falling in the Tier 1 of the regulation, many smaller banks in lower tiers of the regulation would only have to keep records—which does not create a money incentive to follow the rules. Another Dodd-Frank proposed rule is the "clawback" rule that would require firms to recover a bonus seven years later if the employee's actions caused the firm to restate financial results or caused "financial or reputational harm" to the company or if fraud was used to influence the bonus. The rule apparently does nothing to ensure that the money will be there seven years later. Moreover, it will be years before any of these remedial rules become final regulations, and no one is betting on what will survive the lobbying.

The state business corporation laws and the state executive departments responsible for administering them must be reinvigorated, particularly with regard to the Business Judgment Rule and the Fiduciary Responsibility Rule. Clear, enforceable, uniform state rules should be adopted that cannot be circumvented by lawyers, judges, court trustees, or masters appointed by the court.

There must be major reform of the offshore tax shelters that shunt billions of dollars earned by American companies and individual citizens out of the domestic tax base and throw the burden on the middle class. An article on December 4, 2015, listed the top ten companies with the "largest stockpiles of indefinitely reinvested foreign earnings"[52] or foreign IRE. For more than a generation, U.S. corporations have been moving offshore various operations in order to replace higher paid Americans with lower paid foreign workers and to dodge U.S. income taxes. The top corporate tax bracket in the United States is only 35%, and it is not unreasonable to expect these corporations that have reaped so many benefits from the American system to pay this fair share.

Ten U.S. corporations hold $742 *billion* in foreign IRE. These monies are *profits,* not revenues, and none of the cash has been taxed by the United States even though the corporations that made the profits are incorporated and managed here. GE and Microsoft, for example, held $119 billion and $108 billion, respectively, in foreign IRE, and these amounts equaled 18% and 61% of the respective companies' total assets. Apple held $91.5 billion in IRE, equal to 31% of total assets. That so many billions of dollars in U.S. corporation profits should go untaxed is an outrage.

Pharmaceutical manufacturer Pfizer recently announced a plan to merge with Ireland-based Allergan, which would shift the headquarters from New York to Dublin and reduce the "effective" corporate tax rate from 26% to 12.5%. Apple had previously introduced us to the concept of stateless income when it divulged that it had offshored a large operation and thereby avoided paying essentially any tax on billions of dollars of income.

In April 2016, it was reported by a German newspaper that eleven million documents had been "leaked" to the International Consortium of Investigative Journalists relating to a Panama law firm establishing secret offshore bank accounts and other vehicles to shelter monies for hundreds of top government leaders, athletes, politicians, and business titans around the world.[53] Politicians claiming that they are in favor of business-transaction transparency have been shifting millions of dollars to secret offshore tax havens. What is new here is that the actors in the offshore money-handling, money laundering, and tax avoidance schemes include many people in high public office and that the largest havens included places like the British Virgin Islands. This tax abuse by U.S. citizens is easy to correct, requiring only some honest hard work, tight legislative language, a vote in Congress, and a presidential signature.

It is mystifying that financial and business executives and managers responsible for billions of dollars of public investors are not compelled to undergo specialized training in the basic rules of prudent business judgment, fiduciary duty, and ethics; to pass an exam; to be certified; to take twelve hours a year of continuing education; and to be independently regulated by state boards—in the same fashion as private attorneys. It is true that Chartered Financial Analysts do undergo serious training and certification, but they are a small minority.

The avalanche of malfeasance has occurred because of unrestrained greed, ambition, and narcissism in factions (business corporations) and the corrupt relationship among industry, politicians, and government officials that Roosevelt termed a corrupt alliance. Although we will not apply the word "corrupt" to the federal courts, there is plenty of evidence that federal judges, trustees, and special masters have failed to apply the rules of conduct in banking and business in a way that serves justice, punishes the miscreant, and deters future wrongdoing.

Finally, the need exists for an "attitudinal shift" among the American people and U.S. corporations. We address this subject in a later chapter.

---

[1] George Washington, "George Washington to George Mason," 27 March 1779, *The George Washington Papers at the Library of Congress, 1741–1799*, ed. John C. Fitzgerald.

[2] Pub. Law 111-203 of 2010, Preamble.

[3] Andrew Ackerman, "Volcker Criticizes Delay to Namesake Rule," *NYT DealBook*, 19 December 2014.

[4] Id.

[5] Jonathan Weisman and Eric Lipton, "Wall Street Chips Away at Dodd-Frank Rules," *NYT*, 14 January 2015, A-1.

[6] Id.

[7] William D. Cohan, "Regulation Alone Will Not Change Bad Behavior on Wall Street," *NYT DealBook*, 16 March 2016.

[8] Nathaniel Popper and Michel Corkey, "5 Banks Are Still Too Big to Fail, Regulators Say," *NYT DealBook,* 16 April 2016.

[9] "The Savings and Loan Crisis," www.federalreservehistory.org/Events /Detail/View/42. See also, Robert D. McFadden, "Charles Keating, 90, Key Figure in '80's Savings and Loan Crisis Dies," *NYT*, 2 April 2014.

[10] Sewell Chan, "U.S. Faults Regulators Over a Bank," *NYT*, 11 April 2010, Business.

[11] Eric Dash. E. and Andrew Ross Sorkin, "Government Seizes WaMu and Sells Some Assets," *NYT,* 25 September 2008, Business.

[12] Stephen Labaton, "U.S. Regulators' 2004 Rule Let Banks Pile Up New Debt". *NYT*, 3 October 2008, Business.

[13] Floyd Norris, "Regulators Seek Meeting of Minds," *NYT*, 5 June 2004, Business.

[14] Teresa Tritch, "Standard & Poor's Was Let Off Easy," *NYT* Op. Pages, 5 February 2015.

[15] Kurt Eichenwald, "Wages Even Wall Street Can't Stomach," *NYT*, 3 April 1989, Archives.

[16] U.S. Securities and Exchange Commission, "AIG to Pay $800 Million to Settle Securities Fraud Charges by SEC," *SEC Release 2006-19*, 9 February 2009, http://www.sec.gov.

[17] Id.

[18] Gretchen Morganson, "AIG, Where Taxpayer Dollars Go to Die," *NYT,* 9 March 2009, DealBook, http://dealbook.nytimes.com.

[19] "Court-Appointed Lehman Examiner Unveils Report," *NYT DealBook,* 11 March 2010 (includes total nine volumes of court examiner's report).

[20] Peter J, Henning, "Financial Crisis Cases Sputter to an End," NYT DealBook, 4 April 2015.

[21] Mike Whitney, "Lehman Brothers Scandal Rocks the Fed," Counter Punch, 15 March 2010, http://www.counterpunch.org.

[22] "Court-Appointed Lehman Examiner Unveils Report," *NYT DealBook,* 11 March 2010 (nine volume report attached).

[23] "Former S.E.C. Lawyer Pleads Guilty in Dreier Case," *NYT DealBook,* 9 November 2009.

[24] Hedge Fund Lounge, "Hedge Fund Fraud: $291.8 Million Guilty Plea," http://hedgefundlounge.com.

[25] Hedge Fund Lounge, http://hedgefundlounge.com.

[26] Mortgage Fraud Blog, "4 Plead Guilty in Mortgage Fraud Scheme," 28 August 2008, http://mortgagefraudblog.com.

[27] Stephen Labaton and Charlie Savage, "S.E.C. Fines Didn't Avert Stanford Group Case," *NYT,* 18 February 2009, Business.

[28] Alex Berenson and Diana B. Henriques, *"S.E.C. Says It Missed Signals on Madoff Fraud Case,"* *NYT,* 16 December 2006, Business.

[29] Thomas MacMillan, "Controller for Madoff's Firm Gets Time Served," *The Wall Street Journal* (hereafter "*WSJ*") 20 May 2014, C3.

[30] Floyd Norris, "Tyco to Pay $3 Billion to Settle Investor Lawsuits," *NYT,* 16 May 2007, Business.

[31] Accounting Today, "WorldCom Investors to Get $6.1 Billion," 1 November 2005, http://www.accountingtoday.com.

[32] Rachel Louise Ensign, "Regions Financial—Lawsuit Is Settled for $90 Million," *WSJ* Financial Briefs, 20 May 2015, C2.

[33] Ben Protess and Jessica Silver-Greenberg, "U.S. is Seeking Felony Pleas by Big Banks," *NYT,* 10 February 2015, A-1.

[34] Id.

[35] CFTC Release PR7159-15, 23 April 2015.

[36] Jessica Silver-Greenberg and Ben Protess, "J.P. Morgan Faulted on Controls and Disclosure in Trading Loss," *NYT DealBook,* 14 March 2013.

[37] Id.

[38] Rachel Louise Ensign, "J.P. Morgan Chase—Holders Back Pay Plan, But Margin Is Slimmer," *WSJ* Financial Briefs, 20 May 2015, C2.

[39] Michael Corkery and Jessica Silver-Greenberg. "Morgan Stanley Reaches $1.25 Billion Mortgage Settlement," *NYT DealBook,* 4 February 2014.

[40] Peter Lattman, "Galleon Chief Sentenced to 11-year Term in Insider Case," *NYT DealBook,* 13 October 2011.

[41] Christopher Matthew, "Jury Votes to Convict SAC Manager," *WSJ,* 18 December 2013, C-1. Peter Lattman and Ben Protess, "$1.2 Billion Fine for

Hedge Fund SAC Capital in Insider Trading," *NYT DealBook,* 4 November 2013.

[42] Peter Lattman et al., "SAC Capital Agrees to Plead Guilty to Insider Trading," *NYT DealBook,* 4 November 2013.

[43] Christopher Matthews and Aruna Viswanatha, "U.S. Attorney Aims to Dismiss Insider Trading Charges in SAC Capital Advisors Case," *WSJ*, 22 October 2015.

[44] Roger Perloff, "How MF Global's 'missing' $7.5 billion was lost and found," 15 November 2013, Fortune.com.

[45] James B. Stewart, "Boss's Remark, Employee's Deed, and Moral Quandary," 5 July 2013, *NYT* Business Day.

[46] Roger Perloff, "How MF Global's 'missing' $1.5 billion was lost and found," 31 October 2011, Fortune.com.

[47] AFL-CIO, "Executive Paywatch, accessed 12 May 2016, www.aflcio.org/CorporateWatch/Paywatch-2015.

[48] Edward E. Lawler, "Outrageous Executive Compensation: Corporate Boards, Not the Market, Are to Blame," *Forbes*, 9 October 2012, http://www.forbes.com.

[49] Ibid.

[50] Jan Lieder, "The German Supervisory Board on its Way to Professionalism," *The German Law Journal*, Vol. 11, No. 2, 116 (2010), http://www.germanlawjournal.com.

[51] Donna Borak and Andrew Ackerman, "Are You in the Clawback Club," *WSJ*, 22 April 2016, C1.

[52] Kevin McCoy, "U.S. Firms Stockpile More Untaxed Foreign Earnings," *USA Today*, 4 December 2014, 1B.

[53] Michael Schmidt and Steven Lee Myers, "Panama Law Firm's Leaked Files Detail Offshore Accounts Tied to World Leaders," *NYT,* 3 April 2016.

Chapter 11

Infections in Congress

"Those who have been at the expense of purchasing their places [in public office] will be in the habit of repaying themselves... The law which allows this abuse makes wealth of more account than virtue, and the whole state becomes avaricious."
—*Aristotle (c. 350 BC)*[1]

More than two thousand years ago Aristotle attacked the use of private monies to purchase public offices. He described how the public official becomes corrupted by taking on political debts and loses essential virtue, and how the corruption spreads aggressively until the *whole state* become avaricious. There were not enough drachmas in 350 BC to cause Aristotle to imagine the scale of corruption now present in America, but his prediction of the whole state becoming avaricious is quite eerie in its accuracy. Americans always seem interested in the collapse of foreign countries, but blind to corruption and decay of the republic here at home. People are cynical and disgusted with politics, but they do not speak out or protest en masse, as happened in the 1960's and 1970's. I suppose this vacuum itself is what Aristotle meant when he said that the whole state becomes avaricious. The people look to their own possessions, not the quality of public representatives and their governance.

The disease has many facets. It would have been unthinkable thirty years ago for the death of a Supreme Court justice, i.e., Antonin Scalia, to be followed within hours by news broadcasts blaring that "fierce battle lines" had instantly emerged and an entire political party (in this case, the Republicans) was preparing to block the President of the United States from performing his constitutional duty to appoint a successor—because the president is a Democrat. Of course, all new events have to be characterized as fierce battles to sell the infotainment. In the past, journalists would have followed Scalia's death with legal and policy analyses of Scalia's impact during his term and informed speculation regarding possible successors.[2]

The disease in Congress needs to be examined by looking first at the powers and duties assigned to this body by the Founders. Congress enacts all federal laws (statutes) that a majority wishes to enact. The president can veto any statute passed by Congress, but two-thirds of the legislators can override a veto. With respect to presidential appointments, the Senate has the final authority to "advise and consent." The debates at the Constitutional Convention and the writings of the Founders make clear that "advise and consent" have their normal English meaning: the first party, the president, selects appointees for the positions, and the second party, the Senate, can comment to the White House on the fitness of the appointee, provide advice based on its own knowledge of facts, and ultimately hold hearings and confirm or reject the appointment. It is expected and intended that the president may choose a person who does not share the political views of his opponents; he has won the election.

Congress has the power to review and ratify or reject foreign treaties negotiated by the president or his secretary of state. It is a two-step process just as with appointments. Congress can conduct impeachment proceedings with regard to public officials, including judges and the chief executive himself. Congress (the House) appropriates all monies spent by the government. Congress can decide by two-thirds vote to call a convention to amend the Constitution. Two-thirds of the *state* legislatures may force Congress to call a convention. Through its powerful committees, Congress oversees the administration and enforcement of all federal laws and programs. Article I, Section 8, of the Constitution gives Congress a general grant of authority to "make all Laws which shall be necessary and proper for carrying into Execution the foregoing Powers." The Founders did not want important actions to languish for lack of any supplemental legal authority. During the American Revolution the Continental Congress lacked this "necessary and proper" authority, and the war effort suffered.

Congress is gargantuan in size. The Founders knew that legislatures are large and constitute the most powerful body of government, but they may not have foreseen five hundred and thirty-five members. In addition, there are numerous aides to congressmen, committee staff members, the General Accounting Office,

Congressional Budget Office, Congressional Research Service, and the Library of Congress. Congress has powerful committees with special responsibilities for appropriations of money, the regulation of banking, the judicial system, national security, energy, the environment, transportation and interstate commerce, public works, public health, and other vital functions.

Congress undoubtedly possesses sufficient resources to perform all of its duties competently and properly, as the Founders intended.

As recently as in the 1970's the chairpersons of the congressional committees were held in high esteem because of their specialized knowledge in their respective fields and their personal devotion to the particular causes. When issues arose regarding the national defense, federal taxation, and public health or the environment, for example, the chairmen and their staff delved into the issues and were fully capable of meeting and discussing them with experts in the executive branch, industry, and the public. The chairmen and committee members did not need to rely heavily (or entirely) on daily feedings from Washington lobbyists and special-interest groups.

The daily duties of congressmen are straightforward and unambiguous. Members are expected to participate in the proposing, drafting, sponsoring, co-sponsoring, reviewing, holding conferences on, and finally, voting upon legislative bills. Republican Senator Margaret Chase Smith of Maine had a perfect attendance record at voting roll calls.

In a recent editorial, the author Thomas Beck discussed how members of both houses now routinely violate Article 1, Section 5, of the Constitution, that *requires the presence of a simple majority of the membership to conduct business.*[3] Failure to muster even 51% of the members to conduct the business of the nation reveals a shocking lack of discipline and national commitment. It is interesting that some private companies have had attendance problems at board of directors' meetings despite the payment of substantial sums of money for attendance; the solution, for some companies, has been simple: to require the delinquents to forfeit their right to stand for re-election. It is an effective remedy.

The voting public is barraged with 24-hour-a-day infotainment, and yet the most elementary information necessary to evaluate our representatives—the issue-by-issue positions taken on the different bills—is not regularly presented or easily accessible, as it should be.

"Transparency" and "accountability" have not made it even to the threshold of the Capitol Building. For generations, Congress has cloaked its members in veils of secrecy, especially with regard to ethics-and-conduct complaints and proceedings. The current status on that issue is discussed later. If there were a prize given for political hypocrisy in Washington, there would be many contenders, but one clear institutional winner is the U.S. Congress.

In 1958, Congress enacted Concurrent (now Joint) Resolution No. 175, the first Code of Ethics for Government Service.[4] The Resolution states that it should be adhered to by all Government employees, including officeholders. "Officeholders" includes members of the House and Senate, as a researcher for the Congressional Research Service stated in the brief history of ethics codes that he wrote in 2013.[5] This Code was a great step forward; it hit the key points in an unambiguous, straightforward manner. However, it was an unenforceable resolution of Congress, not a legally binding statute.

It stated the following:

- "Any person in Government service" should put loyalty to the "highest moral principles and to country above loyalty to persons, *party*, or Government department."
- The person should give a "full day's labor for a full day's pay." (Compare this to the discussion of members' voting records below.)
- The person should "make no private promises of any kind binding on the duties of office, since a Government employee has no private word which can be binding on public duty."
- The person should "never discriminate unfairly by the dispensing of special favors or privileges to anyone, whether for remuneration or not."
- The person should "expose corruption wherever discovered."
- The person should "uphold these principles ever conscious that public office is a public trust."

If these standards had been met and enforced in the U.S. Capitol, the last half century of American history and politics would have been very different. Founder Alexander Hamilton commented on the nature of human beings when they are tied closely together in a faction or group, such as in a committee or even Congress as a whole. He said:

> Regard to reputation has a less active influence when the infamy of a bad action is to be divided among a number than when it is to fall singly upon one. A spirit of faction, which is apt to mingle its poison in the deliberations of all bodies of men, will often hurry the persons of whom they are composed into improprieties and excesses for which they would blush in a private capacity.[6]

This quotation needs to be studied. Hamilton contrasts what happens when a figure in the public eye takes action *by himself* with what happens when that person is *part of a group or faction*. The individual on his own is more concerned with his reputation, judgment by peers and the public, and possible bad consequences of his decisions. By contrast, a public representative who is a member of a political party or other group is much less conscientious and more prone to "improprieties and excesses" because he is inflamed by the "spirit of faction" that *mingles its poison in the deliberations of all bodies of men.* Hamilton has presented us with a good piece of social psychology—the reasons why legislatures so often abuse their power. (Donald Trump has defied this conventional wisdom by taking the risk of playing directly to the infotainment industry beyond the shelter of his own faction.)

In 1994, a faction of seventy-three Republicans made a flashy entrance into the Capitol and were dubbed the "Freshman Republicans." Freshmen, by nature, have things to learn. This group, however, was ready when it crossed the threshold to announce an agenda to gut environmental protection rules, some of which were pushed through by the most distinguished member of their *own party,* Senator John Chafee. The Freshmen thought the rules were unpopular with industry and that they could solidify their popularity with industry by peremptorily cutting them down. This was one of the first times a group of politicians en masse defied a couple of hundred years of American democratic principles. Where was the reasoned discourse? Where was the independent thinking?

The Freshmen vowed to free industry from health, safety, and environmental constraints that did not pass a hypothetical cost-benefit ratio.[7] Everything was converted into dollars. If the allowable burden of regulation was reduced to 5% of the economy, it would pass muster. Wetlands protection was a prime target even though all competent environmental scientists agree that healthy wetlands are critical to the health and welfare of humans as well as animals. Wetlands are buffers against marine surges—as in New Orleans, and they are the nurseries of marine life that sustain people and many living creatures. Programs are now underway to rebuild wetlands in coastal communities, including New Orleans.

The Freshmen failed. Today, they might not have—a scary thought.

More recently, in March 2015, forty-seven Republican senators sent a group letter to leaders of a nation hostile to the United States—Iran. In the 1970's senators for the most part made up their minds after hearing the arguments pro and con from all sides; political party block-voting was rare to non-existent. By contrast, the Republican Party block warned Iranian leaders not to enter into a deal on nuclear arms limitation with President Obama because the senators would overturn the treaty in the United States Congress. No precedent exists for this outrageous mass breach of the United States Constitution occurring while the president and his secretary of state were still negotiating the treaty. Whatever the flaws may have been in the treaty, the proper recourse was to consult with the president and his secretary of state and await the submission of a final document for deliberation and ratification vote. Article II, Section 2, states that the *president* has the power, "by and with the Advice and Consent of the Senate, to make Treaties, provided two thirds of the Senators present *concur*." "Concur" means follow. It is a two-step process.

In George Washington's day, the Republicans' stunt would probably have earned them a trial for treason—and possible hanging. Today, the Justice Department would have been well within its rights to convene a grand jury to investigate potential criminal violations of various provisions of law on the part of the forty-seven. It was disappointing that the president did not pursue that course to uphold the Constitution against partisan attack.

The fact that the leader of Israel came over to this country in advance and used his extraordinary lobbying power to promote the Republicans' letter makes the whole incident even more repugnant.

The pernicious influence of money has taken a variety of forms in Congress and the political process. The particular schemes change, but the overall modus operandi remains the same. Perhaps the classic scandal was the Jack Abramoff affair that had a number of components and reached into different directions. Indian tribes made a payment of $80 million for political pressure on the Department of the Interior, Indian Affairs, and a showering of bribes and gifts led to the conviction of *twenty* individuals, including lobbyists, government officials at Interior and even the Criminal Division of the Justice Department, two aides of the House Majority Leader (Republican Tom DeLay), and DeLay's colleague, Representative Robert Ney.[8] A draft report of the House Government Reform Committee reviewed daily journals and found 485 lobbying contacts with White House officials (under George W. Bush) in three years, mostly made in person.

Some of the congressmen created an entity entitled "The U.S. Family Network" and used it as a conduit for illegal funds. Russian oil executives gave $1 million to secure DeLay's support of an International Monetary Fund bailout of the Russian economy. Congress *elevated* DeLay to the position of top leadership in the House of Representatives: House Majority Leader. DeLay's colleague, Representative Ney, ultimately admitted that he effectively put his office up for sale to Washington lobbyists. He had been able to direct a multi-million-dollar Congressional contract to one of Abramoff's clients, and in a separate incident he received money to relax the American embargo on the sale of aviation parts to Iran. Abramoff pleaded guilty to fraud, tax evasion, conspiracy, and bribery of public officials. Abramoff's plea agreement (available online) is good reading.[9] The victims of the scandal suffered losses of $25 million.[10]

The House Ethics Committee (officially titled the "Committee on Standards of Official Conduct," but abbreviated "HEC") reprimanded

DeLay for *other* incidents—once for pulling an intellectual-property bill off the calendar after favors were given by an industry group, and a second time for improper use of Federal Aviation Agency resources in an attempt to prevent Texas democrats from fleeing Congress to defeat a quorum on a re-districting bill. HEC reprimands have never had clout. DeLay ultimately resigned from Congress when he was facing a U.S. Justice Department investigation into his involvement in the Abramoff case. The Department never brought that criminal case against DeLay. A separate prosecution for laundering corporate contributions to divert money to elect Republicans to the *state* legislature initially proceeded to a conviction but was overturned on the ground that that action did not constitute a Texas state crime.[11] The fact that DeLay said he had spent $12 million in legal fees over the years to defend ethics and misconduct charges gives us some measure of the fitness of this man for multiple terms in high public office.[12]

On April 4, 2015, the United States indicted Democratic Senator Robert Menendez (New Jersey) for conspiracy, bribery, and false statements to the government. It was alleged that Menendez received thousands of dollars in bribes and items of value from a physician who in return obtained the senator's pressure on government agencies to grant visas for the physician's girlfriends and to end a Medicare billing dispute. Some of the bribe money was allegedly paid to Menendez's legal defense fund entitled "The Fund to Uphold the Constitution."[13] It is reported that Menendez wrote to the Departments of State and Homeland Security in support of two convicted Ecuadorian embezzlers of millions of dollars from a bank, who were opposing extradition from the U.S. Relatives of the brothers gave Menendez $10,000 and the Democratic Party $100,000.[14]

In February 2016, Democratic Senate Minority Leader, Senator Harry Reid, publicly called on Democratic Representative Alan Grayson to drop his race for a senate seat in view of an HEC investigation into his clearly unethical intermixing of private business (as a hedge fund manager for the formerly named Grayson Fund) and public service.[15] Reportedly, Grayson "boasted" in his promotion of the fund, *while a congressman*, that he had traveled to "every country" in the world studying overseas stock markets and fine-tuning an investment strategy that would profit from knowledge of global companies being harmed by economic or political turmoil.[16] The travels were conducted in part as congressional delegations; Grayson even appointed staff aides to his hedge fund positions. Congressmen have disrespected and abused their public offices before, but rarely, if ever, have they reached the point of running a hedge fund while in Congress, using staff aides in the business, exploiting congressional foreign trips to promote the fund, and—while an ethics investigation was pending—campaigning for election to the U.S. Senate.

The current status of committees assigned by Congress to regulate its own members is as follows.

The Senate has a Select Committee on Ethics ("SCE") and the House has the House Ethics Committee ("HEC").[17] The SCE requires that new personnel and members, within 60 days of employment, either attend *one* live session or go online to watch *one* video regarding their compliance obligations and then sign a form and submit it to an Ethics Compliance Officer. The requirement is no more than tokenism. Even private attorneys in the United States not holding the fate of the nation in their hands are required to study for and pass state bar exams (that include ethics) and take continuing legal education courses (including ethics) consisting of twelve hours each year, as specified by the state boards. The boards independently handle complaints against practitioners and impose sanctions for misconduct up to and including disbarment. Serving as a member of Congress obviously involves a different body of knowledge, different skills, and different ethical considerations than representing a private party. Those who enter into this realm owe it to all Americans to be specially trained, precisely as Madison said.

In the House of Representatives in April 2015, *one* congressman, Democrat David Cicilline of Rhode Island, fought for mandatory annual ethics training. The House of Representatives, after much squabbling, appears to have accepted for the first time a rule requiring a single hour of ethics training for *first-year* members only—to catch up with the Senate.

The SCE is supposed to oversee compliance with a federal statute that prevents a member or high staff person from negotiating the terms and conditions of future employment as lobbyists with private industry. The statute is written to exclude contacts made while in office with private employers in the regulated industry if those contacts *precede* the making of an actual offer of employment and the discussion of detailed terms and conditions. Therefore, the private employer simply postpones the offer and detailed terms, and the member and staff person are then free to build their lucrative futures while they are still in public office.

A departed senate member or staff person cannot appear before the Senate or lobby on behalf of a third party seeking "official action" until the passage of two years or one year, respectively, after leaving public service. This ban is circumvented in many ways, including having surrogates in the lobbying firm or trade association make the contacts, or by claiming that the client party is not seeking "official action." The one-to-two-year time period is inadequate anyway; the Canadian ban is five years.

Finally, the SCE makes public Annual Reports that merely list the *numbers* of complaints or allegations dismissed or resulting in some action against a member or staff member during the year. The January 29, 2015 report states that *of forty-five allegations made of misconduct, forty-four were dismissed, and zero sanctions were imposed.* The charged individuals retain their anonymity and have no incentive to reform.

In the House of Representatives, there was optimism when a new ethical body, the Office of Congressional Ethics ("OCE") came into existence in 2008. The OCE was staffed with a handful of independent lawyers under the direction of a former Department of Justice prosecutor, Leo J. Wise. The OCE under Wise initially investigated the widespread practice of inserting earmarks into Congressional bills. Earmarks are authorizations of public funds to be spent for pet projects of congressmen (and their lobbyists) without public bidding. Congressmen obtained campaign contributions in return for the earmarks. The practice was a logical choice for the first wave of investigation by OCE. However, there were intentional flaws in the creation of the OCE. Congress refused to grant it the power to subpoena testimony, which, as any prosecutor knows, is often fatal to being able to build a case. Furthermore, the OCE is an investigative body that can publish findings but not take action. It must refer cases back to the HEC for any action, which historically has meant that the charged individual receives a dismissal or, at most, a letter of reproval.

Nevertheless, even OCE's limited authority has sufficiently threatened members from both parties to prompt a series of attempts to suppress OCE. One bill supported by nineteen Democrats would have prevented the release to the public of any OCE report unless the HEC itself took affirmative action (which it has rarely done).[18] The OCE was under attack in January, 2013, as its reauthorization date approached, and several members' terms expired.[19] Many congressmen have tried to cut the budget and limit the already insufficient powers of OCE, and they have made baseless accusations against it (e.g., racism) that have been rejected by independent watchdogs.[20]

On October 15, 2010, OCE Director Wise announced his resignation—but not before concluding a major investigation of a case of earmarks. In this case, a member of the House Appropriations Subcommittee on Defense solicited and obtained campaign contributions from a lobbying firm representing defense contractors, from the contractors themselves, and from their political action committees (PAC's). There were invitations to dinner. In return, the congressman sent a letter to the Chairman of the Appropriations Committee requesting that certain projects by the contractors be funded publicly. The total value exceeded $14 million. There was nothing subtle about the payoffs. The lobbyist's clients had even prepared a table showing the quid pro quo for each contribution: the campaign contributions were listed in one column, and the contractor projects that the congressman would arrange to be funded with public money were listed in a parallel column. The congressman and his staff declined to be interviewed, and the OEC had no subpoena power. Fortunately, the Justice Department followed up on the OEC referral even though the HEC refused to do so in the face of overwhelming evidence.[21]

According to the HEC and OCE websites (cited above), it appears that since the OCE began work in 2009, the OCE has referred for action to the HEC sixty-one specific cases against named individuals. The HEC has dismissed or closed without any sanction at least 15 cases and issued four letters of reproval, one censure, and one reprimand. Many OCE referrals are unaccounted for, at least in the published reports. The HEC took *no action* when members accepted gifts and filed false reports, but when charged, returned the gift. When a member relied on bad advice from staff and committed violations, the HEC again did not hold the member responsible. In one case, the HEC merely adopted a subcommittee report of the elements of wrongdoing and considered that adoption to be sufficient final action.

A depressing consequence of the legislative deterioration in Washington is that good congressmen have departed in disgust and frustration. More than thirty senators have walked away from their seats since 2010—a record for this 100-person body.[22] Counted among those departing legislators are some veterans who were key supporters of environmental laws (John Dingell, Henry Waxman, and George Miller) and many other well-regarded legislators like Carl Levin, Tom Harkin, Jay Rockefeller, and Evan Bayh. All were disgusted with the do-nothing, acrimonious, self-seeking behavior of the members. Bayh, a centrist, said that after having seen the Senate function properly when he was young and his father was a well-respected senator (Birch Bayh), he could no longer participate in a body where "the people's business is not being done."[23] Bayh noted that, although there had always been political maneuvering, in the past, senators had been willing to put politics aside for the welfare of the country. That is no longer the case.

In February, 2012, Republican Senator Olympia Snowe from Maine announced that she could no longer tolerate the "atmosphere of polarization and 'my way or the highway' ideologies" that have become "pervasive in campaigns and in our governing bodies."[24] This mass of departures is an indictment of America's most powerful branch of government.

One major cause of the decay is the "revolving door syndrome." Staff and top government officials and congressmen leave their jobs to take positions with the industries that they were supposed to be regulating or their agents and associations. This practice makes a sham out of the duty of impartial business regulation. In 2009, in response to the 2008 financial industry implosion, at least *seventy former members of Congress* were lobbying on behalf of Wall Street and financial services firms, including two former Senate and two former House majority leaders, and a former Speaker of the House.[25] *Fifty-six* former Senate and House staff members from the Congressional banking committees went to work lobbying for the financial sector. It is no surprise why the Dodd-Frank Act emerged as it did.

Veteran Massachusetts Representative Barney Frank had top responsibility for financial industry reform legislation. Frank is a brilliant man and an outspoken representative of the people. He exploded in a press statement when a top aide involved in the drafting work accepted an offer to go to work for an industry group representing one of the largest financial companies targeted by the statute.[26] Frank later left Congress.

The revolving-door syndrome has heavily afflicted the Securities and Exchange Commission.

We have mentioned filibustering. Filibustering is the making of prolonged speeches or the introducing of irrelevant material to prevent a bill from coming to a vote on floor. One reason why Congress has been so ineffectual during recent decades (Times columnist Frank Rich called it "comatose") is the puerile practice of filibustering, no longer permitted in the House.[27] The House of Representatives banned filibustering years ago because of the impossible gridlock that would result from allowing any one of 435 members to block legislation by prolonged irrelevant speechmaking. To an objective observer, the whole practice seems completely out of place in our highest legislative body. A filibuster can be halted under Senate rules by a successful cloture vote of three-fifths of the senators (sixty votes). The number of motions for cloture votes (indicating the number of filibusters that needed to be halted) rose from less than seven in the 1960's to 140 in the 2007–2008 Congress (112 motions passed).[28] (Even the cloture vote is somewhat of a farce. It limits the time consumed by the filibusterer to an additional thirty hours after the vote, but a determined majority of senators can still manage to delay the time of final vote for up to two weeks.) [29]

A recent enactment now bans filibusters in the Senate, but only with respect to 1,183 presidential appointments. The bill was in response to a long episode of obstructionism that resulted in approximately thirty appointments by President Obama being blocked without a full hearing. The Senate should have banned the filibuster entirely.

We previously mentioned term limits. A mistake was made in 1787 (see chapter entitled Forming a More Perfect Union) that must be rectified. The consequences of inaction on term limits have been grave.

Legislators have effectively converted public service into private fiefdoms reminiscent of the feudal age. Once a congressman cements relationships with moneyed factions, the system rewards him with longevity in public office. It is in his interest to pander to the same factions year after year, not to examine every bill and every issue with fresh eyes. Republican Senator Trent Lott, for example, held seats in the House and Senate for thirty-five years despite rigid adherence to narrow-minded, sometimes repugnant, ideologies; there were recurrent charges of serious misconduct against him. Lott resigned in 2007, one year into a six-year term, when there was a bribery trial against his brother-in-law and a fear that the Senate was seriously tightening its ethical rules. Segregationist Strom Thurmond held his seat for an astounding forty-seven years; he refused to vacate the seat even when he entered Walter Reed Hospital at age 99 and was clearly unfit. Former Republican Senator Ted Stevens from Alaska held his seat for forty years. It was always easy to predict Stevens' fossilized views on bills dealing with oil drilling (affirmative), and national parks, refuges, environmental protection, and federal regulation of business (negative).

In the past, there have been some distinguished members of Congress who served multiple terms. The sad truth now, however, is that very few members of that quality remain. Many have left in recent years, and the majority of the members who now benefit from the absence of term limits are the persons it would serve the country to remove.

In 1995, bills on term limits initially supported by the Freshman Republicans were drafted in the House and the Senate. The Senate bill would have limited all members of Congress to twelve consecutive years (two terms for senators and six terms for representatives). As a vote approached, the supporters weakened and requested postponement. Two senators, John Ashcroft and Olympia Snowe, refused to agree to postponement. In the end, self-interest prevailed again, and the bills failed.[30]

Republican Senator Jim DeMint from South Carolina said "Americans know real change in Washington will never happen until the end of the era of permanent politicians."[31] A group called "U.S. Term Limits" today advocates a constitutional amendment that would limit a senator to two terms (twelve years) and a representative to three terms (six years). It cites the fact that fifteen state legislatures have term limits, as do eight major cities (for mayors and council members), thirty-seven states (for "constitutional officers"), and the United States Constitution (for the president—two terms).[32] At the time of writing, USTL maintained online a petition and other advocacy materials. This reform is an essential element in any treatment regimen for America.

The current absenteeism rates at Congressional rollcalls are completely unacceptable. They escalate dramatically when a member decides that he or she wants to seek higher office. The member, of course, is still collecting the same salary and has the same important legislative responsibilities. There is widespread agreement that the truism rates of students in public high schools can and must be greatly reduced—and there is an increasing level of joint action to achieve this result. And yet there has been no bipartisan uprising against legislative absenteeism that constitutes a theft of public monies and default of the highest public duties.

GovTrack, a project of Civic Impulse, LLC, has presented data on the absenteeism of legislators during the years before the individual's political campaign and of the campaign.[33] Democrats and Republicans missed 11% to 51% of rollcalls in the year *preceding* a campaign year for the presidency, and well in excess of 50% of rollcalls during the entire campaign year. Minimum attendance standards must be set for rollcalls regardless of the officeholders' personal plans for the future. The 1958 Ethics Code called for a "full day's labor for a full day's pay." Congressmen have certainly made a mockery of this plain-spoken rule of behavior.

The greatest change in politics and Congress since the 1970's has been the money flow. The Center for Responsive Politics (OpenSecrets.org) has compiled and analyzed the money flow, as reported to the Federal Election Commission. There are "Political Action Committees" (PAC's), "Leadership PAC's" (politicians raising money for *other* politicians in the same party to boost their bids for committee chairmanships and top positions), Super PAC's (politicians raising apparently unlimited sums to advocate for or against candidates without giving the money to the candidate directly), and "501(c)(4) dark money outlets" (murky, as the name implies). In the 2012 presidential cycle, the total cost of the election was $6.29 billion.[34] That represents only one part of the legalized money corruption in Washington. The other part is lobbying. In the same election cycle *12,183 lobbyists* spent $3.3 billion.[35] Thus, the total amount of money poured into the political process to influence the result during the two-year cycle reached the astounding sum of $9.6 billion, a figure that exceeds the gross domestic product of a number of countries.

Not one cent of this money went toward improving public education and literacy, building and rebuilding infrastructure, controlling immigration and reviving the system of naturalization, protecting the public health, building renewable energy, reducing greenhouse gas emissions and other pollution, boosting rail transportation, training for jobs, or any other vital public services.

Digging more deeply, we find that both political parties participate in the campaign and lobbying binge. In many instances, a private company or faction gives money to *both* sides in order to create outstanding political debts with the winner regardless of who wins. In other instances, it is obvious why the money goes predominantly to one side, i.e., more labor-union money to Democrats and the vast bulk of financial-industry and oil-industry money to Republicans.

Numerous remedies exist for combatting the disease in Congress and the ailing political system that produces congressmen. Some are already being tested outside America's borders. America's neighbor to the north, Canada, looked south and vowed not to allow itself to succumb to America's disease. Canadians spent years grappling with reform of the political system. Canada enacted an elaborate legislative package that provides guidance for us. The Canada Elections Act and the Federal Accountability Act are the primary statutes. An independent agency, Elections Canada, now manages elections. Much of the information cited below comes from personal communications with, and publications by, that body. Canada has not fully achieved its goals, and disputes have arisen among the political parties regarding some of the methods used, but overall, Canada has taken a major step forward. The United States should consider one or more of the ideas that follow.

Canada has five major political parties and twice that many minor ones. America does not need eighteen political parties any more than Canada does, but there is no doubt that the two-party political system in America has degenerated. We need more and better-quality minds attending to the affairs of the nation. Canada banned political campaign contributions by unions, corporations, and unincorporated associations. If America needs a constitutional amendment to reverse the Supreme Court decisions in this regard, so be it. A number of badly needed amendments have run the course of public education and final ratification in the span of time equal to one four-year presidential term—and we can say that even less good was accomplished during a number of past presidential terms. In Canada, the judicial challenges to the ban were overcome. Elections Canada set an individual private contribution limit of $1,200 in 2012, and only Canadian citizens and permanent residents are permitted to contribute.

Canada recognized that America had failed to clean up campaign financing with limits on campaign contributions alone. Therefore, Canada enacted limits on both contributions to, *and expenditures by,* political campaigns, candidates, and committees. Spending caps are not unique to Canada. One study reports that 25 of 60 democracies have examined and adopted spending caps. Limiting the money influence is especially important because politicians holding office—the incumbents—already have distinct advantages over challengers because of the incumbents' visibility in office and ability to establish fiefdoms. The spending limits in the Canadian general election of 2011 for the top five parties in Canada were $21 million each for four parties and $6 million for the fifth (Quebec)—a fraction of American spending.

In Canada, mandatory, detailed record-keeping of expenditures by candidates, parties, and political action committees is mandatory; the records are submitted regularly to an independent body. Elections Canada posts notice in advance of the amounts allowed for spending, party by party, according to a formula that takes into account voting population and numbers of candidates.[36] Elections Canada presents online a readable set of election financing and spending reports—the Candidate's Electoral Campaign Returns, sorted by candidate, by contributor, and by district. If billions of dollars cannot be spent, then they will not be solicited, and political debts will not be incurred.

Canada adopted a multi-pronged system for *public funding* of elections. The public funding occurs in three ways through: 1) a per-vote subsidy (for the top five major parties that secured, for example, more than 2% of votes cast); 2) partial tax credits for individual contributors on a sliding scale, with the smallest donors receiving the highest credit—to encourage the common man to become involved; and 3) a reimbursement of eligible electoral expenses. The costs of Canada's elections oversight agency—both internal (for running the election) and external (e.g., for TV, print, radio, and world wide web publicity, subsidies, and allowable reimbursements)—were in the range of $300 million.

Canada did not pass a time limit on the incredibly wasteful practice of campaigning. Major crises in America are left unattended for up to two years while candidates, many of whom already occupy public positions, the news media, and the people have their daily plates filled with political-campaign garbage. The Founders would be enraged.

The maximum period allowed for campaigning in the United States should be four to six months.

Another problem is voter apathy and lack of civic engagement. In Canada, a high of 77% voter participation was reached in 1900, compared to 61% in 2011. The statistics are similar to those in the United States. A major national campaign is needed to educate and engage the electorate.

Canada has a Conflict of Interest and Ethics Commissioner with independent authority to investigate complaints and enforce standards applicable to public officeholders and to receive public complaints. The Commissioner also provides compliance advice to officeholders, examines the financial statements filed by the officeholders, and obtains support from an Auditor General and a Director of Public Prosecutions situated outside the Department of Justice. Officeholder education is an important component.

Canada has addressed lobbying as well as campaign finance. Their Commissioner of Lobbying has an "education mandate" and powers of investigation, including the power to compel both oral and written statements under oath from persons with knowledge. Canada's new Lobbying Act imposes a *five-year ban* on post-term lobbying by designated public officeholders. Lobbyists must disclose in monthly reports all communications with officeholders.

The redrawing of political district boundaries in American states—redistricting—has been a major area of disease for years. Members of

Congress always find ways to gerrymander their districts for their own advantage. The public-interest group, California Common Cause, has attacked the problem thoughtfully. It has proposed the use of nonpartisan, independent redistricting commissions, which would hold good-faith public hearings, with the proceedings and maps open to the public. Decisions by the commissions would require a super-majority vote. The commissions would reflect geographic, racial, ethnic, gender, and age diversity.[37]

While this list of reforms is not comprehensive, they all have merit. Treating the disease in Congress and the political process would take America a long way down the road back to health.

---

[1] *Politics*, Bk. II, Ch. 11, 1173.

[2] "Fierce Battle Lines Emerge", *NYT*, 15 February 2016.

[3] Thomas Beck, "Congress Ought to at Least Show Up to Vote," *WSJ*, 24 April 2013, SJ, A15.

[4] House Document 103, 86th Congress, 1st Session, 72 Stat. B12, (July 11, 1958).

[5] Jacob R. Straus, "House Committee on Ethics: A Brief History of Its Evolution and Jurisdiction," Congressional Research Service (CRS 7-5700), 27 November 2013 (italics mine).

[6] Alexander Hamilton, *Federalist Papers, No. 15*, 111.

[7] Michael Arndt ct al., "The GOP Agenda: As Republicans Take Charge in Congress, A Look at the 'Contract with America'," Chicago Tribune, 1 January 1995; http://articles.chicagotribune.com/1995-01-01.

[8] Although Wikipedia is an interactive encyclopedia not to be cited as a general matter, in this particular case the facts are well known, and Wikipedia contains the best overall summary, supported by extensive citations. https://e.wikipedia.org/wiki/Jack_Abramoff. There have been two films as well.

[9] United States District Court for the Southern District of Florida, U.S. v. Jack A. Abramoff, Case No. 05-60204-CR-HUCK, *Plea Agreement*, 4 January 2006, FindLaw.com. http://fl1.findlaw.com/news.

[10] Philip Sheron, "Law Maker Admits He Took Illegal Gifts" and "Ney is Sentenced to 2½ Years in Abramoff Case," *NYT*, 16 September 2006 and 20 January 2007, respectively.

[11] Adam Nagourney, "Texas Court Overturns Conviction of DeLay," *NYT*. 20 September 2013, A12.

[12] Id.

[13] Alexandra Jaffe, "Menendez indictment, 3 girlfriends, 7 lavish trips, more than $750,000," *CNN,* 3 April 2015.

[14] Philip Bump, "Your 2014 Guide to the Scandals Surrounding Senator Bob Menendez," *The Atlantic*, 24 January 2014, http://news.yahoo.com /2014-guide.

[15] Ted Bennett, Deirdre Walsh, and Manu Raju, "Harry Reid Calls on Democrat Facing Ethics Scrutiny to Drop Senate Bid," *CNN*, 2 February 2016, http://www.cnn.com.

[16] Eric Lipton, "Alan Grayson's Double Life: Congressman and Hedge Fund Manager," *NYT*, 11 February 2016.

[17] All regulations, data, and actions discussed regarding the Senate Select Committee on Ethics and the House Ethics Committee are taken from the official Internet websites of these two bodies, except as otherwise noted. See, OCE, http://oce.house.gov; HEC, http://ethics.house.gov; SCE, http://www.ethics.senate.gov.

[18] Sylvia A. Smith, "Ethics Upgrade Cleaning House," *The Journal Gazette* (Ft. Wayne, Indiana), 3 October 2010, http://www.journalgazette.net.

[19] Scott Bronstein, Joe Johns, and Rahel (sic) Solomon, "Congressional ethics investigators could soon be silenced," *CNN Politics*, 3 January 2013.

[20] A leading independent watchdog in Washington on this issue is *Citizens for Responsibility and Ethics* (CREW).

[21] Office of Congressional Ethics, *Report and Findings relating to Peter Visclosky*, No. 09-4486, December 2009, http://www.OCE.house.gov.

[22] Editorial Board, "The Dying Art of Legislating,*" NYT,* 1 March 2014.

[23] Adam Nagourney, "Democrats Reel as Senator Says No to 3rd Term," *NYT,* 15 February 2010.

[24] Jennifer Steinhauer, "Olympia Snowe Won't Seek Re-election," *NYT,* 28 February 2012.

[25] Eric Lichtblau, "Lawmakers Regulate Banks, Then Flock to Them," *NYT*, 13 April 2010.

[26] Id.

[27] Frank Rich, "The State of the Union is Comatose," *NYT*, 30 January 2010.

[28] U.S. Senate, "Senate Action on Cloture Motions—Cloture Voting, United States Senate, 1947–2000," 1 March 2010.

[29] Richard S. Beth and Valerie Heitshusen, "Filibusters and Cloture in the Senate," Congressional Research Service, 13 May 2013.

[30] Katherine O. Seelye, "House Turns Back Measure to Limit Terms in Congress," *NYT*, 30 March 1995.

[31] Mark Preston, "GOP Senators Push for Term Limits," *CNN Politics*, 11 November 2009.

[32] U.S. Term Limits 2013, https://termlimits.org.

[33] Josh Tauberer, "Presidential Candidates Miss Votes," Govtrack.us Blog, 27 October 2015, https://www.govtrack.us/blog/2015/10/27/presidential-candidates-miss-votes/.

[34] Center for Responsive Politics, "Total Cost of U.S. Elections, 1998–2012," Politicians and Elections/Historical Elections, http://www.opensecrets.org/bigpicture/.

[35] Ibid.

[36] Elections Canada, http://www.elections.ca.
[37] California Common Cause, "Redistricting Reform," http://www.commoncause.org.

Chapter 12

Disease in the Executive Branch

"Let me now take a more comprehensive view, and warn you in the most solemn manner against the baneful effect of the spirit of party generally... *The alternate domination of one faction over another, sharpened by the spirit of revenge, natural to party dissension,* which in different ages and countries has perpetrated the most horrid enormities, *is itself a frightful despotism.* But this leads at length to a more formal and permanent despotism. *The disorders and miseries which result gradually incline the minds of men to seek security and repose in the absolute power of an individual; and sooner or later the chief of some prevailing faction, more able or more fortunate than his competitors, turns this disposition to the purposes of his own elevation, on the ruins of public liberty."*
—*George Washington, Farewell Address (1796)*[1]

George Washington's famous Farewell Address is a keen insight into how the "spirit of revenge" between factions that now dominates the political scene in fact leads to despotism—and is itself a form of despotism. These words carry particular weight because they were echoed by Thomas Jefferson, the political rival of Hamilton, in his First Inaugural, where Jefferson passionately denounces "wicked" and "despotic" political intolerance.[2] The evil that Washington and Jefferson detested is a root cause of the disease in the executive branch as well as in Congress.

Washington was being true to himself at the end of his public career by attacking factionalism and by not vaunting some personal achievement of his own on behalf of America. Washington did not sugar-coat his advice. He delivered it "in the most solemn manner." It behooves us to listen.

The background of this address is that Washington had been reading the writings of James Madison, a Founder small in stature and large in intellect; the two men shared the greatest devotion to America, and a defining hatred of profound divisions among the people that destroyed the functioning of the republic, whether they were based on wealth, geographical region, social position, political ideology, or any

149

other factor. The two men were haunted by "moneyed factions" and political factions. Washington prepared a draft of the Address and gave it to Alexander Hamilton to review and polish, but he secured Hamilton's personal promise not to alter its substance or tone. The Address is very consistent, in content and style, with Washington's own letters on the same subject, and there is no reason to doubt that Hamilton fulfilled his promise. Vice President, soon President, John Adams gave a lasting tribute to Washington and this Address by directing Congress to read it aloud at the opening of each session. Congress continued this practice for years, but chose to dispense with it even as its value for the nation increased.

George Washington presents a scary scenario. First comes the "alternate domination of one faction over another, sharpened by the spirit of revenge." This cycle of political domination and revenge in the two-party system is certainly familiar to all of us. It has reached a new height—or nadir—during the Obama administration. Republicans in Congress stepped far over the line of acceptable—and constitutional— behavior in dealings with President Obama commencing on the day he entered office. The episodes involving the Affordable Care Act, finally enacted after decades of failed efforts and upheld by the U.S. Supreme Court, do not need to be revisited here. Washington described a "frightful despotism" arising from the cycle of political revenge.

Despotism is a word that Americans simply do not utter in regard to their own country. We have been brainwashed to believe there are no despots here—that despots are blood-thirsty foreign dictators. That is not how Aristotle defined despotism. Despotism is the oppressive rule of men that displaces the rule of law. The best examples of despotism in America did not occur in the less advanced early stages of the republic, but rather, as Franklin suggested, in the more advanced stages, e.g., Johnson's Vietnam War, Nixon's Watergate, FBI Director J. Edgar Hoover's target list, Joe McCarthy's demagoguery, and the unconstitutional George W. Bush wars. Benjamin Franklin warned us of despotism more than once.[3]

Washington warned that as time progresses, ceaseless factional attacks and divisiveness lead toward a more "formal and permanent despotism." The people yearn for an end to conflict and chaos even if that means allowing the executive in the White House to exercise powers that are well beyond his constitutional prerogative. The delicate balance in a republic is upset. An elected representative who is poised to choose demagoguery over democracy turns circumstances to his own advantage, to his own "elevation... on the ruins of public liberty."[4]

In the 1960's, the Director of the Federal Bureau of Investigation, J. Edgar Hoover, was a classic despot, albeit not at the top level of government. He was pathological, as shown in a book by the former United States Attorney in Manhattan, Frederick A.O. Schwartz, Jr.[5] Hoover secretly spied first on dozens of Americans, then on hundreds. The pretense, like Joe McCarthy's, was national security. While Martin Luther King was crusading for civil rights, Hoover snooped on him. He characterized King as a subversive who should be moved aside; there was a threatening tone in his privately recorded words, as Schwartz indicates. Hoover amassed a huge dossier on Americans from his eavesdropping and spying. The Central Intelligence Agency and the National Security Agency conducted their own abusive and illegal spying programs. Ultimately, Senator Frank Church from Idaho convened a special committee in Congress and exposed the wrongdoing in a celebrated 1976 investigation report.[6] Unfortunately, it failed to become a lasting civics lesson; it was not retaught and relearned. Despotic tendencies do not fade away on their own.

The Nixon Watergate Scandal was a classic case of bloodless despotism. Perhaps the best episodes to examine here are two devastating examples of unconstitutional executive branch war-making. The Founders, for obvious reasons, were well attuned to the war-making issue, and they sharply delineated the powers to *declare* war in Article I of the Constitution (Congress) and to *conduct* war in Article II (the Executive). At the Constitutional Convention George Mason argued that the chief executive could not be trusted with the power to declare war.[7] Hamilton, the so-called conservative Founder, wrote the definitive *Federalist Paper* (No. 69) on this subject. Hamilton was the Founder least likely to limit the powers of the chief executive, and yet he did precisely that with regard to war-making. Hamilton distinguished the American system from the British one in the following words:

The President is to be commander-in-chief of the army and navy of the United States. In this respect his authority would be nominally the same with that of the king of Great Britain, but in substance much inferior to it. It would amount to nothing more than the supreme command and direction of the military and naval forces, as first general and admiral of the Confederacy; while that of the British king extends to the *declaring of war* and to the raising and regulating of fleets and armies.[8]

The Founders officially adopted this distinction in the two articles of the Constitution. Article I, Section 8, states that the "Congress shall have Power to... declare War." Article II, Section 2, states that the "President shall be Commander in Chief of the Army and Navy of the United States." The language could not be clearer. The Founders wanted many minds to deliberate the pros and cons of launching a foreign war, one of the most momentous actions that a nation can take. The Founders anticipated that Congress would grow in size and stature and would be able to hold hearings, determine the true facts, consider international and domestic laws and policies, evaluate the costs of war, and debate the negative consequences of waging war. The Founders explicitly wanted to avoid the risk that a single, elected official might succumb to improper influence, political partisanship, personal bias or ambition, or just plain ignorance and bad judgment.

Long after the end of the Vietnam War, former Secretary of Defense, Robert McNamara, made a film documenting the mistakes made, and lessons learned, during the long Vietnam War.[9] Lesson Number One was to *know the enemy.* Democratic President Lyndon B. Johnson and McNamara had repeatedly violated this rule. Neither man adequately understood the history, culture, military capability, topography, or political status of either North or South Vietnam, where more than 50,000 American soldiers died, and many others were maimed. Our supposed ally, the leader of South Vietnam, was a corrupt despot himself. Johnson's scare tactic of threatening that without full U.S. military engagement, North Vietnam and China might clasp hands, form a monolithic Communist bloc, and take over all of Southeast Asia was pure demagoguery. There was a long history of antipathy between these countries. All signs pointed to a repeat of France's failure to pacify Indochina. Yet Lyndon Johnson refused to heed the lesson. In the later years of the war, McNamara tried to persuade Johnson that they had made a mistake in launching the war, refusing to back out, and misleading the American people into believing that there was a global Communist threat in Vietnam that we must and could eliminate. Johnson would hear none of it.

Here was despotism, pure and simple. At least Robert McNamara, the Secretary of Defense, learned from it and created a record that should have guided his successors in government. The Vietnam War is the only war in which the people forced Congress to repeal its phony declaration of war after the fact.

McNamara was interviewed as part of a George Washington University series. He said: "External military force cannot reconstruct a failed state, and Vietnam, during much of that period, was a failed state politically... It [reconstruction] proved to be impossible."[10]

There are strong similarities in personality and behavior between Lyndon Johnson and George W. Bush despite their allegiance to different political parties. Johnson had overarching hubris. Johnson had demanded that Congress approve the Gulf of Tonkin Resolution (H. J. Res. 1145). However, House Joint Resolution 1145 failed to meet the basic criteria for a declaration of war under Article I, stating that Congress resolved to approve and support the *"determination of the President"* to take necessary measures to repel armed attack against forces of the U.S. and prevent further aggression. In fact, the Constitution grants no authority to the president to make such a determination and no authority to Congress to delegate its constitutional duty. Declaring war must be on a case-by-case process, and that process is assigned to Congress.

Only a generation later, President George W. Bush, blind to the lessons of Vietnam, invaded and occupied Afghanistan and Iraq. He clearly lacked rudimentary knowledge of—and apparent interest in—the long history of conflicts among religious and tribal sects and the reasons why a U.S.-inspired democratic government could not be grafted onto existing regimes. A much nearer neighbor of those countries, the U.S.S.R., had failed in its twelve-year-long Afghanistan offensive. Bush named his war the "War against Terror," affirming his ignorance of McNamara's prime lesson to know the enemy; he could not even identify the enemy. The U.S. went ahead with the invasion and the bombing that destroyed human beings and buildings, roads, pipelines, and other infrastructure that had to be rebuilt, of course at U.S. expense. When some Americans challenged the absurdly low cost estimates for the war, the pro-war faction mocked them publicly and presented estimates in the low billions of dollars, not trillions.

The Watson Institute for International and Public Affairs, at Brown University, prepared a credible, independent cost estimate. It takes into account costs that the Department of Defense and Congress repeatedly fail to include: interest on capital spent, medical rehabilitation of veterans, both mental and physical, and so forth. As of June 2014, this combined cost estimate was $4.37 trillion, the equivalent of the entire U.S. federal budget for an entire year.[11] That amount of money could have purchased many items essential for an attack on America's systemic disease.

In Bush's war the American troops occupied one town and region after another, only to have them retaken by the enemy. There have been so many turnovers, still ongoing, that it is difficult to keep count. This year, more than 300 Iraqis died in a single day from suicide bombers—15 years after the U.S. invaded and occupied the country declaring that they were bringing democracy, i.e., the rule of law, into a completely foreign place. The result was the conflagration of Islamic extremism and violence that analysts not surprisingly predicted.

In 2015, U.S. planes reduced to rubble a well-known hospital used by Doctors Without Borders, the largest hospital facility in the Afghanistan region. Bombers took five separate runs to pulverize the building and kill all inhabitants that had not been able to flee: doctors, staff, and patients remaining inside.[12] It was an atrocity that should have put an end to this multi-trillion-dollar, fourteen-year exploit, but pro-war factions, lobbyists, the military-industrial complex, and the chief executive, simply refused to halt. Civilian control of the military was always a key part of the American design, and it was embraced heartily by General Dwight David Eisenhower, the Supreme Allied Commander of World War II, when he became president. His famous "Military Industrial Complex Speech" is excerpted below.

Demagoguery played a much greater role in the months leading up to Bush's war than Johnson's war. Bush campaigned for his war with all sorts of demagoguery; it is reflected in the resolution he obtained from Congress (below). Omitted from Bush's public campaign were policy and strategic analyses prepared by the Departments of the Army and State that detailed the *negatives* of invading and occupying the Muslim countries.[13] A conflagration of anti-western radical Islamism was predictable—and predicted.

Before launching his war, Bush could have spent an hour or two watching McNamara's "Fog of War" film to learn the basic lessons from Vietnam. Bush's rebuffing of the world's top U.N. official responsible for identifying and controlling weapons of mass destruction (Hans Blix) was the classic act of a despot.

The Congressional resolution on Iraq (J. Res. 114) mimicked the Tonkin Gulf resolution. It purported to authorize the president in the most general terms to use armed forces "as he determines necessary" to defend U.S. national security and enforce U.N. Security Council resolutions. It was a blank check, and the two specific references it did make—to threats to U.S. national security and to the U.N. resolutions—were a fraud. J. Res. 114 was explicitly predicated upon the existence of "large stockpiles of chemical weapons and a large scale biological weapons program" and a link between Iraq terrorists and the World Trade Center attack of September 11, 2001—neither of which was true.

On January 17, 1961, before both the Johnson and Bush wars took place, Republican President Dwight Eisenhower gave his now-famous speech on the threat of the military industrial complex, an alliance of factions. He was one of the most popular presidents in history because he was the Supreme Allied Commander, who combined military, personal, and diplomatic skills that enabled the free world to win a world war. Eisenhower also strengthened and built America in a number of important ways as president. No one was more qualified to speak on the subject of the threat from a military-industrial complex. Eisenhower had strong similarities to George Washington—in character, experience, deep loyalty to America, sincerity in all aspects of his life, and abhorrence of factions. Eisenhower said, in part:

In the councils of government, we must guard against the acquisition of unwarranted influence, whether sought or unsought, by the military-industrial complex. The potential for the disastrous rise of misplaced power exists and will persist. We must never let the weight of this combination endanger our liberties or democratic processes. We should take nothing for granted. Only an alert and knowledgeable citizenry can compel the proper meshing of the huge industrial and military machinery of defense with our peaceful methods and goals so that security and liberty may prosper together.[14]

The speech has strong echoes of Thomas Jefferson: "*Only an alert and knowledgeable citizenry* can compel the proper meshing of the huge industrial and military machinery of defense with our peaceful methods and goals *so that security and liberty may prosper together.*" Eisenhower made the essential connection between preventing and controlling factions and maintaining liberty and national security. He readily grasped the advice of Madison and Washington on that point and the lesson of Jefferson that ultimately only an alert and knowledgeable citizenry can save the republic from becoming a despotic government.

---

[1] George Washington, Farewell Address (1796), Avalon ("Address") (emphasis mine).

[2] Yale Law School, Lillian Goldman Law Library, *The Avalon Project—Documents in Law, History and Diplomacy, The Inaugural Addresses of the Presidents* (hereafter "*Avalon*"), http://avalon.law.yale.edu/18th_century/fed10.asp.

[3] *Notes*, 17 September 1787, III, 1651–52.

[4] Address.

[5] Frederick A. O. Schwartz, Jr. and Aziz Z. Huq, *Unchecked and Unbalanced: Presidential Power in a Time of Terror* (New York: The New Press, 2007).

[6] United States Senate Select Committee to Study Governmental Operations with Respect to Intelligence Activities, United States Senate, Books I–III (1976).

[7] *Notes*, II, 1352.

[8] *Federalist*, No. 69.

[9] Errol Morris, *The Fog of War: Eleven Lessons from the Life of Robert McNamara,* Sony Pictures Classics, 2003.

[10] George Washington University, *Episode 11—Vietnam, Interview of Robert McNamara,* http://www.2.gwu.edu/.../interviews/.../ mcnamara.

[11] Watson Institute for International and Public Affairs, "Summary of Costs of War Iraq, Afghanistan, and Pakistan FY 2001–2014, Billions of Current Dollars," June 2014, http://watson.brown.edu/costsof war/.

[12] Joseph Goldstein and Eric Schmitt, "Errors Cited in U.S. Airstrike on Doctors Without Borders Hospital," 24 November 2015, *NYT*. Margherita Stancati, "U.S. Airstrike Kills 19 at Doctors Without Borders Hospital in Afghanistan," 3 October 2015, *WSJ*, World.

[13] James Fallows, "Blind into Baghdad," *The Atlantic*, 1 January 2004, http://www.theatlantic.com.

[14] Dwight David Eisenhower, "Military-Industrial Complex Speech," 17 January 1961, *Public Papers of the Presidents, Dwight D. Eisenhower, 1960*, 1035–40, http://coursesa.matrix.msu.edu/~hst306/documents/indust.html.

Chapter 13

Disease in the Judiciary

"It is difficult to speak about judges, for it behooves us all to treat with the utmost respect the high office of judge... but there is a need that those who go wrong should not be allowed to feel that there is no condemnation of their wrongdoing."
—*Theodore Roosevelt, Autobiography (1913)*[1]

The Founders intended to insulate federal judges from politics by having them appointed for life by the president with the Senate's advice and consent, and by creating only one rigorous procedure for a judge's removal from office—impeachment by Congress. Until the latter part of the twentieth century this system held up well. Cracks appeared when President Richard Nixon nominated to the Supreme Court two politically conservative men (Haynsworth and Carswell), who possessed mediocre professional qualifications and who were tarnished by bias. There was no lack of well-qualified candidates in the country, acceptable to Republicans and free from unacceptable bias, as Nixon later proved by nominating Harry Blackmun, who was unanimously confirmed.

Although an arm of the American Bar Association (of attorneys) reviews federal judicial candidates for fitness, it has never been a deep or comprehensive review. The result is that the system of judicial appointment is now plagued by political deal-making and revenge-seeking, just as George Washington described. Unfortunately, the failings do not end with the appointment. In recent years more and more federal court rulings were easily predicted based on the political ideology of the judge when he or she was nominated and of the nominating president. Achieving the goal of a non-political federal judiciary has been frustrated.

The disease is particularly evident in the U.S. Circuit Court of Appeals for the District of Columbia Circuit, a key federal court that holds the axe over many government programs. The damage recently has been manifested in the striking down of agency regulations affecting business and industry. The longstanding rule was that courts would give deference to the expertise of federal agencies and not take it upon themselves to eliminate regulations because they did not agree with them. The standard for upsetting a regulation is that the regulation be clearly contrary to the law or simply arbitrary, that is, not supported by facts and the law. Some of the courts' most egregious overstepping of their bounds has been with regard to rules issued by the SEC post-2008 to inject more transparency and shareholder democracy into the workings of corporations. The reasoning expressed in the D.C. Circuit opinions for upsetting the rules has itself been arbitrary and ridiculous. The judges were Republican appointees.

One well-respected, nonprofit environmental group undertook a partial study of court decisions applying the National Environmental Policy Act.[2] In twenty-three cases decided by George W. Bush appointees the pro-environment plaintiffs won only four times, a success rate distinctly below the average percentage for all Republican appointees and far below the average for all appointees from both parties in 217 cases (44%). This limited study lent support to the hypothesis that the judiciary had become increasingly politicized and therefore in violation of Article III of the Constitution. It is disappointing that other nonprofit groups and foundations have not followed up with further studies. Honest, evenhanded adjudication is at the heart of a democratic nation. It is likely that nonprofits tread carefully to avoid upsetting their corporate funders; the public good suffers.

It is also not a good sign that an article in the *Wall Street Journal* reported that a national Republican group is spending heavily on judicial campaigns at the state level (where judges are popularly elected, not appointed) and is prompting state judges "to get more involved in their campaigns as they seek to hold on to their seats."[3] This is contrary to the enlightened path of "merit selection" of judges.

The slate in Congress needs to be wiped clean of political debts that skew these judicial appointments and set in motion a cycle of political revenge. Both the president and Congress need to strengthen the process of good-faith screening of judicial candidates for merit, temperament, and lack of bias. More assistance can be obtained from bipartisan panels of private lawyers and retired judges. These reforms will only succeed if both sides appreciate that political revenge is extremely damaging to the republic as a whole. As President Franklin Roosevelt found out, a lifetime appointment cuts two ways. Roosevelt was unhappy that judges appointed from Democratic Party slates were not upholding some of his New Deal reforms. FDR's plan to "pack the court" failed—as it should have.

The federal judiciary is the branch where there has been the least disease; and because it *is* the last resort for justice, America's treatment regimen should include steps to return the presidential-appointment and Senate-approval process to higher ground.

---

[1] Theodore Roosevelt, *Theodore Roosevelt: An Autobiography* (New York: MacMillan, 1913), 56, Bartleby.com (1999); www.bartleby.com.

[2] Jay E. Austin et al., *Report—Judging NEPA: A "Hard Look" at Judicial Decision Making under the National Environmental Policy Act*, (Washington, DC: Environmental Law Institute, December 2004), http://www.eli.org/researchreports.

[3] Joe Palazzo, "More Judges Forced to Hit Campaign Trail," *WSJ*, 13 October 2014, A4.

Chapter 14

A Process for Democracy Reform

"The people are the only censors of their governors... Cherish therefore the spirit of the people, and keep alive their attention. Do not be too severe upon their errors, but reclaim them by enlightening them."

—*Thomas Jefferson to Edward Carrington (January 16, 1787)*[1]

The Founders could not anticipate all the ways in which future generations would veer off course or the magnitude of their errors. However, many of their apprehensions were astoundingly accurate. The *Federalist Papers* and their letters show that the Founders knew it was impossible to write a constitution that would address all contingencies. Neoconservative attempts to prevent flexible interpretation of the Constitution seem more and more ridiculous as one digs deeply into the actual writings of the Founders. On the one hand, Jefferson understood that the people would make errors, lose their focus, lack enlightenment, and fail to censor their governors. He pleaded for society to "cherish the spirit of the people" and find ways to rehabilitate them.

On the other hand, Alexander Hamilton, Jefferson's political rival, *said almost exactly the same thing:*

> To balance a large state or society... is a work of [such] great difficulty, that no human genius, however comprehensive, is able by the mere dint of reason and reflection to effect it... The judgments of many must unite in the work; EXPERIENCE must guide their labor; TIME must bring it to perfection; and the FEELING of inconveniences must correct the mistakes which they *inevitably* fall into in their first trials and experiments.[2]

Hamilton's capitalization of certain words and emphasis on "inevitably" show that he, borrowing a passage from the English philosopher David Hume, strongly believed there would need to be creative democracy reform in the future *and* that this should be a task for "many" minds, not any elite group or faction. That Hamilton accepted an alternative mechanism for calling a constitutional convention (by the state legislatures) further demonstrates that he would have had an open mind with regard to one or more of the model processes for reform presented here.

George Washington expressed the same sentiment:

> The power under the Constitution will always be in the People. It is entrusted for certain defined purposes, and for a certain limited period, to representatives of their own chusing [sic]; and whenever it is executed contrary to their Interest, or not agreeable to their wishes, their Servants can, and undoubtedly will be, recalled.[3]

If we look back at constitutional amendments, we see that they are suited for very specific reforms, e.g., the right to vote, term limits for the president. Some of the parts of America's treatment regimen fall in this category, but others do not. Nevertheless, we should not succumb to false notions that constitutional amendments are just too cumbersome and time-consuming. It depends on whether a solid grass-roots movement in favor of the amendment has been developed, and it has educated and motivated the people. Smart legislators would rather be of help to their constituents than not. Where the proper foundation has been laid, amendments have become law in no more than the four years of a single presidential term of office—and many such terms have passed along with a lot less having been accomplished.

Fortunately, various processes for democracy reform have been the subject of attention and experimentation here and abroad. At Stanford University in California, James S. Fishkin is the Director of the Center for Deliberative Democracy and the author of books on a proprietary process known as Deliberative Polling® (DP).[4] This process has been applied with various collaborators, such as MacNeil/Lehrer Productions, to explore the difference between *uninformed* public opinion and *informed* public opinion. Deliberative Polling is specifically designed to help overcome the dual evils of demagoguery and the education deficit and to improve the quality of decision-making. DP works as follows:

A questionnaire is developed on the subject matter in question. A random, representative sample of citizens is selected, formed into groups, and presented with a balanced set of briefing materials. Trained moderators are assigned to each group. The groups prepare specific questions to be answered by experts and policymakers. (I have referred to independent commissions.) The groups then hold moderate discussion and deliberation. The members attend a plenary session of the whole, and all the participants present the key questions to experts and policymakers. A final questionnaire is compiled with the *informed opinions* of the participants. Not surprisingly, there are substantial changes between the initial and final questionnaire responses. The results are analyzed and released to the news media.

The Deliberative Polling process has been used in the European Union and China, as well as in the U.S. and Africa a total of twenty-two times.

The DP process is somewhat reminiscent of the original citizen's assemblies of Ancient Greece, the birthplace of democracy. Citizens' assemblies have been the subject of Internet "blogs."[5] They are composed in various ways and clothed with various powers. They are not media-choreographed affairs like the misnamed "town-hall meetings" held during American presidential election campaigns. They often have a substantial budget and professional staff; they can call witnesses and hold hearings; they can obtain documents; they can obtain honest expert advice and interpretation; and they can deliberate and make recommendations that may result in initiatives, referendums, legislation, or constitutional amendments.

One group in Europe, Challenge for Europe, has reacted to the reported presence of 16,000 lobbyists in Brussels, a political cancer spread from America.[6] The idea is to reform the Brussels-EU situation with the help of citizens' assemblies. At the time of writing, the bureaucratic and lobbying weaknesses of the EU have become so severe that the United Kingdom has improvidently voted to pull out. That would not have happened with Deliberative Polling. Citizens' assemblies would have helped.

At one point, people in the United Kingdom had the idea of adopting a written constitution and using a citizens' assembly as part of the process to develop it.

When government fails badly, as in the case of McCarthyism, a logical alternative is to call for an independent commission composed of eminently qualified and widely respected persons. Senator Margaret Chase Smith suggested this approach in her Declaration of Conscience. The most famous independent commissions around the globe have had very different purposes than reforming the American republic. In the case of South Africa, extensive negotiations led to the enactment of a law (the 1995 Promotion of National Unity and Reconciliation Act) to abolish apartheid and establish a Truth and Reconciliation Commission headed by Desmond Tutu. This commission was much more of a backward-looking judicial body than a forward-looking democracy-reform body. However, it did play a critical role in allowing the country to go forward by holding numerous hearings at which victims of apartheid revealed the horrible truth of the past and achieved a measure of catharsis. Revealing the truth and broadcasting it among the people was critical for reconciliation and progress.

Most of America's independent commissions have been retrospective—investigating past calamities, such the World Trade Center attack, and creating a detailed set of findings of fact, as a court would do, that might lead to remedial action by the legislature for the future. The quality of work performed by the bipartisan 9/11 Commission was impressive: the "9/11 Commission Report—Final Report of the National Commission on Terrorist Attacks Upon the United States."[7]

Two political scientists in Canada, Matthew Mendelsohn and Andrew Parkin, have proposed joining independent commissions with citizens' assemblies as a means of cutting through the ignorance and demagoguery and enabling the citizens to do what Thomas Jefferson expected them to do. The Parkin-Mendelsohn ideas have been published in various journals.[8] Citizens' assemblies, without commissions, have been used in British Columbia, New Brunswick, and Ontario.[9] In British Columbia, a citizens' assembly came together in the following manner. Some 15,800 invitations were mailed to BC citizens. In order to function, the members needed to be literate and otherwise capable and willing to deal with civic issues. The selection of the final 160 members was quasi-random; it was balanced for gender, location, and age, but not for socioeconomic status or ethnicity, although a few indigenous peoples' representatives were added. The proposition on the table was specific: whether the voting procedure in BC should be changed to a ranking of all candidates rather than the casting of votes for a single individual. The proposition obtained sufficient support to stir up interest in the legislature, but it failed to pass by a significant margin.

Aside from the merits of the proposition, there were problems of voter apathy (turnout is in the same range there as in the U.S.) and inadequate public education. The process itself was defective. The public information in the form of advertisements was very superficial; it failed to identify all the pros and cons of the proposal, and, fatally, it did not lead the voters to believe *that they would be impacted by the outcome or give them a compelling reason to support reform.* That is the key. Voters must believe that the measure on the slate for a vote would correct a wrong that is both unacceptable and of major consequences to the republic and themselves.

In America we have many more resources to accomplish democracy reform than any other country—a cause for optimism. It has been desperately frustrating to watch the republic being swept down the road to civic decay and yet not to have our well-qualified academic institutions, institutes for politics and government, centers for democracy reform, and nonprofit foundations jump in to disperse the demagoguery, educate the people and their representatives, and develop remedies. It was not difficult for me to research and identify a dozen likely institutional participants for an American rescue mission.[10] A cautionary note is that some nonprofits are subtly, or not so subtly, biased in their work by their corporate funders, ideological supporters, and demagogues here and there; they would have to be disqualified. We need many "open minds" dedicated to this mission, as Hamilton said.

At the state level in America procedures exist for the people to push reforms forward. We should understand them. A patchwork of "popular initiatives" and "referendums" serves the purpose of giving the people a direct voice in reforms when their legislatures have failed them or refused to carry forward an initiative. In some cases, the process provides for interaction and collaboration between the legislature and the people. California has led the way. It uses direct initiatives, known as Propositions. It was not an act of the legislature that compelled containers to bear labels identifying carcinogens, but California Proposition 65. These state initiatives cannot serve as federal statutes with nationwide effect, but they can spur multistate and national actions, and in this particular case it was not feasible for the container and retail sales industries to do business *without* labelling all containers in interstate commerce.

There are two types of initiatives: direct and indirect. In a direct initiative, a body of citizens drafts and circulates a petition—often with assistance from a state agency—for signatures by registered voters; if the requisite number of signatures is obtained, the initiative is submitted to the electorate for a direct vote (a plebiscite). In an indirect initiative, the petition is referred to the legislature so that it can decide *first* whether to take action. If there is no action by the legislature or the action is partial, the petition may still go forward as a proposition to the electorate.

Twenty-four states in the U.S. have initiatives. Michigan is a leader among the states in indirect initiatives. It is still surprising that twenty-six states have no initiative process at all. This gap is a loss for democracy.

All fifty states have legislative referendums in which the state legislature can seek public approval or disapproval of a controversial law. Twenty-four states have popular referendums that enable the electorate on their own to approve or disapprove of a law. The rules for initiatives and referendums vary among the states with respect to the number of voter signatures required on the petitions (sometimes expressed as a percentage of votes cast for governor in the last election) and the number of votes cast in order for the measure to pass. The National Conference of State Legislatures maintains an online table showing the current status of initiative law in all states and a great deal of information regarding how initiatives and referendums work as the people's way of bypassing dysfunctional legislatures.[11] Legislative redistricting is examined.

A drawback to initiatives is that, because they often affect wealthy special interests, those entities can and do outspend the reformers in the campaign and thus bias the results. In one recent initiative, insurance and health care companies were affected, and *each* spent more than $50 million during the campaigns. These millions of dollars taint the democratic process.

The 1960's and 1970's still provide us a good roadmap for participatory democracy. The republic is failing because too many fundamental rules and principles of a democratic republic have been violated for too long. We need to explore multiple ways of saving America, in the same way as a team of physicians faced with a systemic disease.

---

[1] Carrington letter, Introductory Quotations.

[2] Hamilton, Federalist No. 85, Mentor, 526–27.

[3] George Washington, "To Bushrod Washington," 10 November 1787, collected in The Library of America, *The Debate on the Constitution: Federalist and Antifederalist Speeches, Articles, and Letters during the Struggle over Ratification,* (New York: Literary Classics of the United States, Inc., 1993), Part One, 305, 306–07.

[4] See, http://cdd.stanford.edu/what-is-deliberative-polling. Carnegie Mellon University has also been involved. http://hss.cmu.edu/pdd./about/index.html.

[5] www.http://citizens-assemblies.net/spip.php?article301.

[6] www.http://challengeforeurope.blogactiv.eu.

[7] National Commission on Terrorist Attacks, "9/11 Commission Report—Final Report of the National Commission on Terrorist Attacks Upon the United States" (New York: Norton, 2004).

[8] Understanding Society, "Citizens' Assemblies," 23 April 2010; http://understandingsociety.blogspot.com. Participedia, "British Columbia Citizens' Assembly on Electoral Reform," 16 September 2009, updated 27 September 2013; http://participedia.net. Matthew Mendelsohn and Andrew Parkin eds., *Referendum Democracy* (New York: Palgrave MacMillan 2001); Paul Howe, Richard Johnston, Andre Blaise eds., *Strengthening Canadian Democracy* (Montreal: Institute for Research on Public Policy 2005), Ch. 7. William Cross, ed., *Democratic Reform in New Brunswick* (Toronto: Canadian Scholars' Press 2007).

[9] Id. Much information was collected by the nonpartisan agency, Elections BC.

[10] The Miller Center for Public Affairs at the University of Virginia; the UVA Center for Politics; the Harvard Kennedy School Institute of Politics and Ash Center for Democratic Governance; the University of Tennessee Howard H. Baker, Jr. Center for Public Policy; the University of Wisconsin–Madison

School of Public Affairs; the Stanford University Center for Deliberative Democracy; the Princeton University Center for the Study of Democratic Politics; the Harry S. Truman Center for Governmental Affairs at the University of Missouri–Kansas City; the Brennan Center for Justice at the New York University School of Law; the Annie Casey Foundation; the Johns Hopkins Carey School of Business Joint Program for Masters in Business Administration and Masters in Government; the National Constitution Center; Carnegie Mellon University.

[11] National Conference of State Legislatures, "Chart of the Initiative States," accessed 23 May 2016. www.ncsl.org.

Chapter 15

A Crusade Against Ignorance

"I think by far the most important bill in our whole code [of laws] is that for the diffusion of knowledge among the people. No other sure foundation can be devised for the preservation of freedom and happiness... Preach, my dear Sir, a crusade against ignorance; establish and improve the law for educating the common people. Let our countrymen know that the people alone can protect us against these evils [ignorance, prejudice, and poverty]."
—*Thomas Jefferson's Letter to George Wythe (1786)*[1]

In 1786, the year *before* America was founded, Thomas Jefferson declared that establishing and improving "the law for educating the common people" was the *only* sure foundation for the preservation of freedom and happiness. In a single sentence, the author of the Declaration of Independence set a clear national priority: the universal education of the common people, by law, not by circumstance, according to standards that he and the other Founders articulated. The law in question was a Virginia bill, but there was no doubt from Jefferson's writings and those of his colleagues that this was a national priority, and that the fate of the two inalienable rights—liberty and happiness—hung in the balance.

Obviously, the new republic had many urgent priorities when it was formed. This makes it all the more significant that Jefferson sent his eloquent plea for a "crusade against ignorance" to George Wythe in 1786. Furthermore, Jefferson emphasized that the people alone can protect us against the evils of ignorance, prejudice, and poverty. Legislators cannot be trusted with this function on their own. They have a propensity to want to make their mark elsewhere. Every first lady in the White House in recent memory has devoted her personal time and attention to schools, literacy, and early learning. And yet, as we will see, the public education system in America has not been improved in scope or quality—and, in fact, it has fallen behind that of other nations. There has been more political hypocrisy associated with public education in the United States than with any other program.

Many politicians proclaim their support, but when it is time to vote on public appropriations, the politicians look elsewhere. When the U.S. economy dipped, the first thing that some governors axed (specifically, in Pennsylvania) was the funding of libraries, early learning programs, and the disciplines that build statesmen and democracy—the liberal arts and humanities. Teaching civics had already been cut. Meanwhile teachers' unions, politicians, school boards, school administrators, parents, and academics never ceased to quarrel among themselves.

Jefferson founded the University of Virginia and supported the Virginia education bill that was the subject of his letter to Wythe. He became a member of the American Philosophical Society (Franklin's creation) and commissioned the Lewis and Clark Expedition from Missouri to the Pacific. Knowledge, learning and hands-on experimentation and invention were Jefferson's daily sustenance. In his 1818 statement to the Commissioners of the University of Virginia, Jefferson, like Madison and Washington, emphasized the importance of education in *civics and the liberal arts* for a proper understanding of our citizenship duties to our neighbors and our country, and for the formation of statesmen, legislators, and judges.[2]

Jefferson wrote: "The basis of our government being the opinion of [i.e., held by] the people, the very first object should be to keep that right."[3]

The way to keep the people's opinion "right" is through education and enlightenment. If the people become inattentive to public affairs, if they fail to censor their governors, Jefferson said, "you & I, & Congress & Assemblies, judges & governors shall all become *wolves.*"[4]

Jefferson had strong support from his colleagues. In his Eighth Annual Message to Congress, President Washington renewed his call for a national university that would teach youth "from every quarter" the "science of *Government.*"[5] For him, the liberal arts went hand in hand with civics.[6] His national university is impractical in America today, but the purpose can be achieved through appropriate curriculums at schools and colleges across the nation.

In his Inaugural Address, President John Adams declared that education of the common people is the "only means of preserving our Constitution from its natural enemies, the spirit of sophistry, the spirit of party, the spirit of intrigue, the profligacy of corruption."[7] In a sentence, Adams captured the urgency of education.

What, then, is the current state of public education in America? The truth is not difficult to discern, although there has been a great deal of demagoguery obscuring the facts and forestalling necessary reforms. Well-established independent bodies assess the state of education in America year by year. We will consult them, but first there is one telling anecdote. An English professor and humanities-education advocate from Harvard, Yale, and Columbia Universities, Verlyn Klinkenborg, wrote an article for *The New York Times* Sunday Review: "The Decline and Fall of the English Major."[8] He pointed to a report by the American Academy of Arts and Sciences finding that the teaching of humanities "has fallen on hard times." It is not coincidental that this major academic shift has coincided with an appalling decline in the quality of America's representatives and business executives. Humanities is the field that encompasses literary expression from the time of the Middle Ages forward—it makes us human.

At Pomona College in 2013, 16 students graduated with an English major out of a student body of 1,560, "a terribly small number," as Klinkenborg says. The changes have been vast and swift. In 1991, 165 students graduated from Yale in English; in 2002, 62 had that major. As most people know, the undergraduate colleges at Harvard and Yale have never ranked their performance by numbers of jobs obtained in the first year after graduation. Graduate schools may do that, but not the college. And yet even these institutions are failing. The point of secondary and college education is to develop the *whole* student and provide benefits to society as well by producing that pool of wise and good citizens Madison envisioned. Klinkenborg commented on the teaching of writing and literature:

> That kind of writing—clear, direct, humane—and the reading on which it is based are the very root of the humanities, a set of disciplines that is ultimately an attempt to examine and comprehend the cultural, social, and historical activity of our species through the medium of language... What many undergraduates do not know—and what so many of their professors have been unable to tell them—is how valuable the

most fundamental gift of the humanities will turn out to be. That gift is clear thinking, clear writing and a lifelong engagement with literature.[9]

As Klinkenborg says, "a technical narrowness, the kind of specialization and theoretical emphasis you might find in a graduate course, has crept into the undergraduate curriculum." We depend on primary and secondary schools, followed by colleges, to develop in the students a base of literacy, knowledge of western civilization and democracy and the role of citizens in this republic, appreciation of the arts and humanities, lessons of history and geography, a moral character, and more. "Technical narrowness" and particular expertise can and should be part of the second step in the learning process—a superstructure that can only stand upon this foundation.

The history of education in America is maddening. In the 1960's, we discovered the disproportionate benefits of early learning. Children who received the benefit of programs like Get Set in Philadelphia and the federally funded Head Start moved forward much better than children without early learning. As the populations of racial and ethnic minorities and children from poor neighborhoods increased, the urgency of early learning *increased*. And yet a half-century later, in the wake of 2008, state governors and politicians defunded early learning programs (and public libraries). In Pennsylvania, the governor and his cronies threw their weight instead behind indiscriminate shale-gas leasing and drilling. Fortunately, this trend was halted by angry voters in 2014, and a new governor has been installed who is an ardent supporter of public education.

The City of San Antonio, Texas, with many children and many in poverty, has bucked the educational cutbacks.[10] There was a proposal to increase slightly the local sales tax to finance more preschool. Slightly more than half the state's four-year-olds are enrolled in a state-funded program. However, the state preschools do not meet standards for class size or staff-to-pupil ratios. Nationally, only 28% of four-year-olds and 4% of three-year-olds are enrolled in state programs.[11]

The Annie Casey Foundation ("ACF") is a pioneer in early learning. ACF reported that: 1) achieving grade-level proficiency in reading is an essential step toward increasing the number of children who succeed academically, graduate from high school on time, and "do well in life and the workforce," and 2) children who do not read proficiently by the end of the third grade are four times more likely not to graduate.[12] In 2011, *82%* of low-income-family fourth-graders were below "proficient" in reading; and in Hispanic, African-American, and Native American communities, the percentages were higher.[13]

The ACF has been supporting an Atlanta, Georgia, project, the Dunbar Learning Complex, that brings together better teacher training, programs involving the parents and the community, anti-poverty programs, and the teaching of "reading, writing, respect and resolution" in the early years. It is a recipe for success. The most successful programs in the field of education, including those dealing with truancy and graduation rates, have been multifaceted and involved a team approach with parents, teachers, administrators, state and local agencies, and the courts.

In Union City, New Jersey, decaying schools were in imminent threat of a state takeover. The community is poor, with many Hispanics needing language education in both Spanish and English. A new administration came in. There was a major effort to improve cooperativeness and mentoring among the teachers, to increase the level of attention paid to individual students, to teach respect and unity (partly with a dress code), and to raise the standards regarding lateness, rudeness, and bullying. At the Woodrow Wilson School, the administration developed a program for outreach and integration with arts institutions that in 2014 won the school a National Blue Ribbon (only eleven schools in New Jersey won this honor).[14]

As at Dunbar, there was a strong emphasis on teaching the lessons of mutual respect, interdependence, and collaboration. The third grade teacher tells her students that her classroom is a pie, a vital community; when the pie is cut into slices, the community is fractured; it loses its wholeness and strength. Thus, she teaches ethics and civics on a mini-scale appropriate for third graders. The overall goals are to build character and teach the students to think.

In Providence, Rhode Island, the Mayor is trying to "close the 'word gap'"[15] with a program called "Providence Talks." Caseworkers visit parents in low socioeconomic brackets (which includes many for whom English is a second language) at their homes and teach them the importance of *talking* to very young children and that there is a pronounced positive difference between those who use many words in an upbeat manner as opposed to communicating merely sharp, negative, disciplinary words. The principles date back to 1980's studies by child psychologists at the University of Kansas, Betty Hart and Todd Risley. The movement has spread to Cambridge, Massachusetts, and many municipalities, and it has been supported by President Obama and Hillary Clinton.

There is also some good innovation in charter schools.

All of this movement is in response to the following. The nation's educational report card is assembled by the Department of Education, National Center for Education Statistics, and the National Assessment of Educational Progress (NAEP).[16] To obtain the full picture for 2013, for example, one must read the report card and the ACF interpretation. The document ranked thousands of students in the fourth, eighth, and twelfth grades at thousands of schools around the country for proficiency at mathematics and reading. A student is proficient in reading when he or she draws conclusions and makes evaluations from the text (in the old days this fell under reading comprehension). Literary and informational texts are used. There are four levels: Below Basic, Basic, Proficient, and Advanced. Minor improvements in fourth and eighth grade performance were overshadowed by the final result: *only 34%* of public school students were reading at the proficient level. The picture for math is essentially the same: 34% proficient in grade eight and 41% proficient in grade four.

Some schools had proficiency rates as low as 17%. Racial differences are pronounced. California and states in the southern half of the country stretching all the way to, but not including, Florida need the most improvement. The immigration factor is huge, as we shall see.

The method of evaluation of twelfth-grade students differs in some respects. Despite some recent improvement in graduation rates, there is no sign of significant improvement in reading or math. In fact, reading is a bit worse now than in the first assessment done in 1992. Reading proficiency hovers at 38% and math at 26%.

In higher education, the Organisation for Economic Co-operation and Development's "Education at a Glance" is quoted as ranking the United States nineteenth out of twenty-eight countries in graduation rates, an inexcusably poor performance in a country with as many material advantages as the U.S.[17]

International studies show that, in addition to more teacher collaboration, there must be more rigorous teacher training and certification, and that teacher performance must be much more closely and objectively monitored. A report released on September 10, 2014, has found the U.S. to be slipping behind comparable, developed nations in "college completion and educational mobility."[18] Americans have always been proud of educational mobility—the increase in educational achievement of second- and third-generation immigrants. The data now suggest that the rate of upward mobility is slipping. Again, huge demographic changes play a large role. It remains true that obtaining higher education is associated with higher levels of earnings, better health, more community engagement, and more trust in government, institutions, and other people—all factors that America needs.

Americans' addiction to technology is pervasive in our society and especially harmful for our youngest citizens. One study found that children under age six spend an average of two hours a day viewing screen media versus thirty-nine minutes reading and benefiting from others reading to them.[19] The American Academy of Pediatrics has strongly recommended against television for children under two because a baby's need for interaction with a human parent or caregiver at that age is critical to healthy development.[20] The studies are in agreement that screen media, even programs deemed educational for children, do not provide the benefits of reading by an adult. If computers were a magic solution to lagging performance, we would be seeing an entirely different set of statistics for American students.

Another issue is that of class time and length of the school year that President Obama has addressed. As any parent knows, in recent years there has been runaway inflation in the number and length of school breaks. The number of class sessions each week has decreased. Compressing two sessions into one is always a loss. Students are young people; all people have limited attention spans.

Pennsylvania law requires a minimum of 180 days of school during the year, equal to 990 hours at the secondary school level or 36 weeks of 5-day-a-week school. A calendar year consists of 52 weeks.

Therefore, there can be as many as 4 months a year in which a student is out of school. This is an enormous loss, scholastically and in other ways. Other countries, especially in Europe, require more classes over a longer period of the year and shorter breaks.

One small private-sector initiative in Philadelphia is "Reach Out and Read." It was founded in 1989 by pediatricians and early childhood educators on the premise that parents and children visit their pediatricians regularly and have respect for, and confidence in, the doctors. According to Dr. Trude Haecker at Children's Hospital, 96% of children five years old or younger visit a pediatrician at least once per year. In this program, the doctors impress upon the parents the critical importance of early reading and provide appropriate books. In Boston, Dr. Mark Vonnegut (MV Pediatrics Health and Wellness Center) is proactive with his young patients and their parents across a broad spectrum of wellness initiatives that improve learning. Classes are held to discuss "unplugging" kids and parents, and returning to basics, reconnecting with nature, and so forth.[21]

We cannot discuss educational performance and ignore immigration. The last census was in 2010, but the level of immigration (legal and illegal) is so high that the Bureau has issued new estimates. Total U.S. population was estimated to be 316 million. The *foreign-born* population increased from14.1 million in 1980 to 31.1 million in 2000 to 42.4 million in 2014.[22] The post-World War I waves of immigration that set the record for decades have now been eclipsed.

It is difficult to estimate the numbers of illegal immigrants. They conceal their existence. The Census Bureau states that it "applies factors." There is no doubt that the number is huge. The federal government's Immigration and Customs Enforcement ("ICE") appears to be in state of breakdown. At the time of writing, some 167,000 convicted criminal aliens with final orders for removal were still at large in the U.S.[23] Deportations have been *decreasing* instead of increasing. In 2013, ICE freed 36,007 convicted criminal aliens from detention while awaiting the end of deportation proceedings, in addition to a separate batch of 8,000 individuals against whom no charges were brought.[24]

I have personally seen the illegal border-crossing. I visited southwest Arizona near the Mexican border and saw lines of Mexicans illegally crossing the border in the canyons at night carrying their sacks. I also saw hundreds of ICE vehicles parked uselessly in lots or cruising the interstate roads.

This crisis is real. While there are many ramifications socially, our focus here is on America's civic breakdown. America has a duty to limit immigration to the point where representative democracy can function and immigrants can become naturalized citizens, fulfilling their role under the law. No one benefits from the charade now existing. The coining of a new politically correct term—undocumented person—makes a mockery of the social contract upon which the republic is based. It is a two-way street with mutual obligations and benefits. To foster an uneducated, mostly illiterate subculture of people lacking the ability or will to participate in the democracy as full citizens violates the fundamental principles and feeds America's system disease. It should also be upsetting to millions of immigrants who entered this country legally, became naturalized, and worked to give their offspring the opportunity to prosper.

I doubt many Americans have ever attended an old-fashioned naturalization proceeding in federal court. I have. A U.S. District Judge first addressed the key criteria, such as compliance with the law, obtaining English literacy, a commitment of loyalty to the republic and the Constitution, and learning our system of representative democracy and how to participate in it. The judge then delivered in the simplest terms a summary of *what it means to be an American*. The experience was similar to the extremely moving, dramatic monologue in the National Constitution Center amphitheater. There were tears in many eyes at the end of both events.

In 1995, Democratic Representative Barbara Jordan from Texas, the first African-American to deliver a keynote address at the Democratic National Convention, chaired the U.S. Commission on Immigration Reform. On February 24, 1995, she testified on behalf of the whole Commission before the Subcommittee on Immigration and Claims, House Judiciary Committee, U.S. House of Representatives. She advocated reasonable restrictions on immigration; making citizenship and naturalization more central to the process; strong and evenhanded enforcement of immigration at the borders and within the country; detention and deportation of criminal aliens; and an interlocked, public-private, computerized system to verify the status of all immigrants. She opposed giving public benefits to illegal immigrants. Few who have heard Barbara Jordan speak at a formal event have ever forgotten it—her marvelous eloquence and command of the language, her presence, and her overriding love of America and the fundamental principles. In the more than twenty years that have passed since her testimony, Americans have yet to follow *any* of her recommendations.

Congresswoman Jordan said:

> We on the Commission believe strongly that it is in the national interest for immigrants to become citizens for the right reasons, not the wrong ones. We want immigrants to be motivated to naturalize in order to vote, to be fully participating members of our polity—to become Americans.[25]

Attempts have been made to measure the rate of civic assimilation by immigrants. Assimilation has become a loaded word. Assimilation does not mean erasing or losing ethnicity, but gaining American citizenship. No democracy (or any other form of government), to my knowledge, has succeeded in attaining Jefferson's inalienable rights *without citizenship*. Education takes time and resources; not having education takes no time, consumes a great deal of resources, and destroys the fabric of democracy. Civic assimilation is measured by whether immigrants become U.S. citizens through naturalization, achieve the education we have described, become informed and vote, join a military service, attend political meetings, contact a political representative or a newspaper, support a candidate, or participate or urge a friend to participate in citizens' petitions, referendums, or movements. There should be more indicators.

The rate of civic assimilation is far below an acceptable level. U.S. employers have definitely not distinguished themselves by their exploitation of cheap labor and their encouragement of a worse-than-lax attitude toward citizenship. Barbara Jordan's Commission was a model of reason and fidelity to the Founders. Americans have a second chance now to repair the system that alone can bring us toward the attainment of our inalienable rights and restore democracy.

[1]Thomas Jefferson, "From Jefferson [in Paris] to George Wythe, 13 August 1786," Founders Online. See also, *Thomas Jefferson–Writings* (New York: The Library of America, Literary Classics, 1984), 857.

[2] Thomas Jefferson, *Report of the Commissioners for the University of Virginia* (4 August 1818), collected in *Thomas Jefferson–Writings* (New York: Literary Classics of the United States, Inc., The Library of America, 1984), 457.

[3] Jefferson, "From Thomas Jefferson to Edward Carrington," 16 January 1787, http://founders.archives.gov/documents/Jefferson/01-02-0047.

[4] Carrington letter (emphasis added).

[5] George Washington, Eighth Annual Message (7 December 1796), *George Washington–Writings* (New York: The Library of America, Literary Classics of the United States, 1997), 978, 983.

[6] George Washington, "To Alexander Hamilton" (1 September 1796), id., 960.

[7] John Adams, Inaugural Address, Avalon. See also www.teachingAmericanhistory.org.

[8] Verlyn Klinkenborg, "The Decline and Fall of the English Major," *NYT*, Sunday Review, The Opinion Pages, 23 June 2013.

[9] Id.

[10] "Start them early," *The Economist*, 22 September 2012, 40.

[11] Id.

[12] Leila Fiester, Annie E. Casey Foundation, "Early Warning Confirmed: A Research Update on Third-Grade Reading" (2013), Executive Summary. Also, "Double Jeopardy: How Third Grade Reading Skills and Poverty Influence High School Graduation," AECF (2012), www.aecf.org.

[13] Id.

[14] Union City Public Schools, http://www.union-city.k12.nj.us.

[15] Margaret Talbot, "The Talking Cure," 12 January 2016, The New Yorker, 38-47.

[16] Department of Education, National Center for Education Statistics, Nation's Report Card, http://www.nationsreportcard.gov.

[17] Reuters, "Higher Ed. Report: U.S. falling behind in the college competition," 10 September 2014, quoting from Organisation for Economic Cooperation and Development's "Education at a Glance," and OECD's Andreas Schleicher.

[18] Id.

[19] Seattle Children's Hospital Research Foundation, https://www.seattlechildrens.org/.

[20] PBS Parents: Children and Media—TV and Kids under 3, http://www.pbs.org/parents.

[21] http://www.gotomypeds.com.

[22] Karen Zeigler and Steve Camarota, "U.S. Immigrant Population Hit Record 42.4 Million in 2014," September 2015, Center for Immigration Studies, http://www.cis.org. Hereafter CIS. U.S. Census Bureau, *Annual Estimates of the Resident Population by Sex, Race, and Hispanic Origin for the United*

States and Counties, April 1, 2010 to July 1, 2013: 2013 Population Estimates, American FactFinder, http://factfinder2.census.gov.

[23] CIS.

[24] Jessica Vaughan, "ICE Document Details 36,000 Criminal Alien Releases in 2013," May 2014, CIS.

[25] U.S. Commission on Immigration Reform, "Testimony of Barbara Jordan before the House of Representatives Committee on the Judiciary, Subcommittee on Immigration and Claims," 24 February 1995, http://www.utexas.edu.

Chapter 16

Following Franklin

"Much of the strength & efficacy of any Government in procuring and securing the happiness of the people, depends on opinion, on the general opinion of the goodness of Government, as well as the wisdom and integrity of its Governors."
— *Benjamin Franklin, Constitutional Convention (September 17, 1787)*[1]

"Our debates were to be… conducted in the sincere spirit of inquiry after truth, without fondness for dispute, or desire for victory."
— *Benjamin Franklin, Autobiography*[2]

Benjamin Franklin, like Jefferson and Washington, was concerned that, in order to secure the happiness of the people, more would be needed than having a great constitution. Continual teaching, learning, and applying of the fundamental principles would be necessary. In his last speech at the Constitutional Convention (excerpted above), Franklin distilled three important thoughts into one sentence: 1) that the purpose of government is to secure the happiness of the people, 2) that much of the strength and efficacy of government in achieving this goal depends on *the people having a positive opinion of the goodness of government,* and 3) that the people's representatives, their "Governors," must always possess wisdom and integrity. The first principle was well established by Aristotle, Rousseau, and the other Founders. The third principle was well established by Aristotle and Madison. The second principle—a positive opinion of the goodness of government—is the focus of this final chapter. There is no better mentor on this subject than Franklin.

In a democratic republic we cannot divorce ourselves from government. The government must be regarded as an extension of ourselves, for so it is. To attack or detest our government is the equivalent of national suicide. We retain ultimate political authority to censor the governors—to alter or abolish any part of government that ceases to serve or promote the public good. If the people do not have a positive opinion of the goodness of government, it means that the people have failed in their duties as citizens. Thus, the remedy for America must include shifting the public attitude. We need "attitudinal shift."

Franklin was a charismatic group leader for civic causes. He could charm the nobility of France, Netherlands, and Spain one moment, and the next moment recruit journeymen civic inventors from Philadelphia's Elfreth's Alley for his Junto Society. Franklin selected the Junto members from a wide variety of trades and professions, from different social classes, and from different age groups. This is one clue to Franklin's and the Junto's success. The Junto was composed of approximately ten people, not much different in size from a committee in Congress or the executive committee of a company, foundation, or the president's cabinet (the heads of the departments). The Junto personified the ideal of Charles Pinckney at the Convention of a mostly egalitarian society where no one had too much, and all had a sufficient amount.

Franklin established *and enforced* a rule of conduct that all debates at the Junto would be "conducted in the sincere spirit of inquiry after truth, without fondness for dispute, or desire for victory."[3] These phrases mean that within the Junto Society the qualities of sincerity, good thinking, loyalty to the common good, teamwork, and mutual respect were winners, and demagoguery and narcissism were losers.

An interesting footnote to this story is that a man named Benjamin Vaughan (occasionally "Vaughan") prompted his friend Franklin to write his (Franklin's) autobiography. He wanted to preserve for future generations Franklin's accomplishments and his public spirit. Vaughan considered it important for future Americans to know that a person's origin (social class and family holdings) does not determine his potential as a human being to achieve happiness and success across a wide realm of human endeavor. The Junto members were filled with energy, curiosity, civic spirit, and respect for each other and their leader. Vaughan wanted Franklin to be a role model for all Americans because, *without mentors*, Vaughan said, people tend to abandon their patriotic efforts, to consider their struggle hopeless, and to fall back on simply taking their place "in the scramble of life, or at least making it comfortable principally for themselves."[4]

One of Franklin's other rules was that each member should make a private effort to establish a new club or society following his own particular civic, philosophical, or natural-science interests. Five or six additional clubs were founded in this way. Franklin knew that the benefits of incubating civic institutions were great for everyone, including the members of the Junto. Public service and the attitude that comes with it can become contagious. Most of us who have participated in public service or charitable work know this to be true. Nevertheless, we must not underestimate demagoguery, greed, political divisiveness, and narcissism; under the wrong circumstances, they can gain the upper hand.

Voluntary service programs have been studied. The conclusions have been that while they often do great good for both recipients and volunteers (consider Habitat for Humanity), a broad and lasting attitudinal shift cannot come into existence solely through voluntary charitable organizations. Those who volunteer are most often the ones who do not need attitudinal shift. Furthermore, America is a long way from the more benevolent age of Franklin, Washington, Madison, Morris, Bingham, Mather, and Meriwether Lewis and William Clark. The gaps among people are wide, and there are too many of them. The only way that we can achieve attitudinal shift is through a universal, mandatory, national service program for young people (18–25 years of age).

Universal service breaks the cycle of narcissism—self-absorption, a narrowing of perspective. U.S. District Judge Holwell was correct in the insider-trading case when he ruled that a terrible virus was raging through Wall Street; the problem is that he did not have the tools to defeat it.

In the 1960's President John Kennedy had a good sense of the ills of America. He summoned Americans to become engaged in public service and to measure their lives by what they have done for others and the larger environment. Two national organizations were born under Kennedy and Johnson: The Peace Corps and Volunteers in Service to America (VISTA), now part of AmeriCorps. President Obama has made a similar appeal. Few of us who have participated in these organizations (two years of service in the former and one year in the latter) claim that we have made enormous differences in the lives of those in need. We accomplished a little good here and there, but the lasting impact was on ourselves.

Many of us gained a new perspective. Sometimes we were pointed toward career changes and lasting changes in our perspectives. We learned *empathy,* a cornerstone of healthy democracy. Empathy and sympathy are derived from the same Greek roots except that the prefix for the former means "in" and the prefix for the latter means "with." When we have empathy, we stand in the shoes of someone else— someone different from ourselves. When we have sympathy, we stand *with* them in their loss, grief, or state of need. Empathy is the stronger word of the two; that is what we must seek in order to turn America around, in order to produce attitudinal shift.

Of course, AmeriCorps and the Peace Corps have their flaws. Neoconservative politicians never cease to pick away at them—as if far more grotesque flaws did not exist in the spheres of business, politics, and plutocracy they inhabit. Universal service is a powerful antidote to corrosive bigotry, factionalism, narcissism, and greed.

There is a broad range of service opportunities in America: teaching languages and literacy (including financial and civic literacy); mentoring the youth; greening the inner cities; developing renewable energy facilities upon which America can always rely regardless of what happens elsewhere in the world; assisting public health and infectious disease programs and programs for the elderly; rebuilding blighted communities; providing legal services for the indigent; volunteering for food banks and community-supported agriculture programs; serving in the nation's parks and refuges; providing natural-disaster relief; developing fine arts and performing arts programs in partnership with schools and needy communities; and so forth. The list is long.

For years, the City of Philadelphia has had two mural arts programs for primary and secondary schools—one with paintings, and one with handmade mosaic tiles. The projects are thematic, which means that students are learning American history and environmental science along with art—and developing a great sense of pride and accomplishment. These projects and what they represent in Philadelphia cast a wonderful glow in the city.

In 2012, a Veteran Job Corps Act was introduced in Congress that would have employed veterans in conservation, resource management, and historic preservation projects around the country. The National Parks Association had an estimate of *$11 billion* of work that needs to be done and has been deferred. The bill failed. The Association and veterans' groups will try again. All of the models for universal service accept military as well as civilian service.

The closest we have come to actual consideration of universal service was when, in 2013, the Universal National Service Act (H.R. 748) was introduced. The Act would have applied to every citizen between the ages of 18 and 25, and would have established a two-year period of service. The president would have been authorized to identify the forms of civilian service. An amendment could have required the president to follow the recommendations of a bipartisan board of six or eight individuals. The bill, like its predecessors, died.

Some of the bills have sought no more than an investigation of the *feasibility* of universal service. Even those bills have been blocked by factions in Washington. Neoconservatives have led the attacks. They claim that universal service is subversive—"socialist training for compliant workers" or a plot by the United Nations to erase American identity by brainwashing our youth with "concepts alien to the United States Constitution."[5] This is McCarthy talk. One well-known Washington, D.C., foundation went so far as to say that universal service programs violate the independent spirit that the country was founded on. A century ago Theodore Roosevelt answered that claim by reminding us that there was a time for "rugged individualism"—when the west was being opened—but that that time had passed, and rugged individualism had become no more than a means to self-enrichment at the expense of others.

Democratic Representative Jim McDermott of Washington and seven other members of Congress sponsored a universal service bill in 2009. McDermott was a medical doctor who served in Africa with the U.S. Foreign Service and had a distinguished record of public service. The preamble of H.R. 1444 of 2009 captured the spirit of universal service: A more engaged civic society will strengthen the Nation by bringing together people of diverse backgrounds and experiences to work on solutions to some of our Nation's major challenges.[6]

The Center for Deliberative Democracy at Stanford University has discussed the issue of citizenship in the twenty-first century and spoken favorably of a limited period of mandatory public service encompassing a wide range of activities, including literacy and education. The Center has said that strictly voluntary service "fails to instill a sense of civic pride and duty in our citizens" and that a mandatory program would "help citizens understand and respect responsibilities of belonging to a society as well as enjoying its benefits."[7] Universal service teaches civics. It has been used by many countries. The notion that compulsory service is un-American is absurd.

There are many pathways to attitudinal change. Ironically, Americans have made admirable progress in achieving positive attitudinal change among many young people. Take a look at preschool, primary school, and even some secondary school programs, and you will find empathy and bonding that did not exist fifty years ago. We can be proud of the creativity and high purpose that underlies those changes. America, however, is in a state of civic breakdown, a level and type of national crisis not previously encountered—although depicted with enormous sensitivity and wisdom by the political philosophers, Founders, and their greatest political descendants. Franklin and the other Founders would certainly have sounded the alarm and set in motion a national movement to reclaim the republic. They would have explored a range of alternatives. We have much to learn from them. One thing is sure. None of these mentors to Americans would have settled for the course that leads to national suicide.

---

[1] Benjamin Franklin, Madison *Notes*, III, 1651–52, (Sep. 17, 1787).

[2] Benjamin Franklin, *Autobiography of Benjamin Franklin*, http://www.benjaminfranklinbiography.net, VII, 54–5.

[3] Benjamin Franklin, *Autobiography of Benjamin Franklin*, http://www.benjaminfranklinbiography.net, VII, 54–5.

[4] Benjamin Vaughan, "Letter to Benjamin Franklin," 31 January 1783, collected in *The Autobiography of Benjamin Franklin*, http:www.ushistory.org/franklin/autob/page35.htm (a project of Independence Hall Association), Pt. 2, 35.

[5] Charlotte Iserbyt et al., "Uncle Sam Wants You, Your Sister, and Your Girl Friend or Wife," http://www.newswithviews.com, 11 November 2003.

[6] H.R. 1444 of 2009, Sec. 2.

[7] The Center for Deliberative Democracy, "Citizenship in the 21st Century," Stanford University, www.http://cdd.stanford.edu/docs2007.

Index

Acknowledgements

I thank all those persons and institutions that have believed in and supported this undertaking, and two persons in particular without whom the manuscript would never have reached the stage of publication: first, Stephanie Beavers of Stephanie J. Beavers Communications, who has performed as editor, adviser, and executive director to a person who is much more comfortable and happy immersed in history, principles, and writing, and second, Nancy Biddle, who understood my goals and designed a magnificent cover.

A second-career writer needs a home where the Muse will impart her wisdom and the people will offer personal help and creature comforts as needed. The following gave me that type of moveable, daytime home: the Luddington Library in Bryn Mawr, Pennsylvania; the Hothouse Café at the Bryn Mawr Film Institute; the Philadelphia Athenaeum; the University of Pennsylvania Lippincott Library; and the Jamestown (Rhode Island) Public Library.

My friends and family steered me away from shoals more times than I can recall. Thank you Ellen, Austin, and Cynthia, and Elaine, my wife, whose daily listening quenched my obsessive need for hearing how the words and episodes would fare outside my own head.

About the Author

Bradford Whitman graduated *magna cum laude* from Harvard College with a B.A. in English and with various academic awards, and from the University of Pennsylvania Law School with a J.D. degree. He served as a VISTA volunteer in Detroit after the 1967 riots, and in 1971, he joined the U.S. Department of Justice, Land and Natural Resources Division, in Washington, D.C. For eight years he practiced law as a trial attorney and also became assistant chief of the section established to represent the new Environmental Protection Agency and other federal agencies. Mr. Whitman handled a wide variety of civil and criminal environmental cases in federal courts across the country; he testified before Congress regarding a major investigation of a nuclear power plant, and he was close to the legislative process during enactment of the 1970's environment laws. The Attorney General nominated Mr. Whitman for the Rockefeller Public Service Award for his work in a landmark water pollution case.

Mr. Whitman was a partner successively in two Philadelphia law firms, taught legal writing, and served as counsel to the second firm for professional ethics before leaving to arbitrate complex environmental cases through a dispute-resolution organization in New York.

Mr. Whitman has written numerous legal briefs for district and appellate courts, one textbook (*Superfund Law and Practice*) published by the American Law Institute, journal articles, and op-eds. In the spring of 2013, he taught a college course in "Environmental Politics." His 1970's Washington experience during the last period when America was resilient in the midst of crisis led him to investigate and write on American history and civics (as originally defined). He currently resides in Wynnewood, Pennsylvania, with his wife. Mr. Whitman can be reached at: bfwhitman2@gmail.com.

Made in the USA
Columbia, SC
18 May 2017